CONTENT

1 DIGGING INTO COMPOST

You can not fail at composting. Is not that a beautiful thing to understand at the onset of a job? The organic thing will rust regardless of what you're doing. Fuss over it every day or dismiss it for weeks; it does not matter. Thus, dig in and revel in the procedure!

This chapter summarizes a couple of stipulations, briefly introduces the soil food web, and provides you a fast description of cold and hot composting procedures. The rest of the chapter covers a number of the numerous advantages of compost and composting.

Welcome To The Planet Of Compost

The decomposition of organic matter is a critical biological process that's ongoing in each corner and cranny of the planet. Composting is a way that you replicate nature's procedure, speeding up it if you choose, to finally benefit from a creamy mound of soil-enhancing compost to your own landscape.

A valuable, soil-like chemical, mulch is a combination of decayed and decaying organic matter that enhances soil structure and supplies nutrients for crops.

If compost is the last product of your home attempt, everything, then, is humus? Compost and humus are conditions that are frequently used interchangeably, even though there are subtle differences. Have you ever seen a stroll in the forests and discovered dropped leaves to spy a rich coating of the soft, sweet-smelling, shadowy ground? That is humus, which will be included in a well-decomposed animal and plant thing. Resembling dark coffee grounds, hummus is lightweight, aromatic, and spongy in texture, so permitting it to carry water.

What equipment and tools that you will need

You do not need to obtain plenty of things to start composting. In reality, you might begin with nothing over that old spade propped in the corner of the garage or shed. But it is much simpler -- and more interesting -- using a couple of well-chosen implements, like a pitchfork and mulch thermometer. I explain the most helpful tools to boost your composting expertise after this chapter. The set is short; therefore, no need to stress in case your wallet is lean!

You might also have questions regarding dirt bins. Are you needed? No, but based on containers, utilize space effectively, give a clean look, and assist you to keep moisture and warmth inside a heap of an organic thing, finally producing compost quicker. Some container designs do a fantastic job of deterring pests, even if that is a concern in which you reside.

The way that works

Composting works excellent once you combine up the ideal mixes of organic matter and living conditions to the soil microorganisms and invertebrates doing all of the decomposing work.

It might be simple to overlook that dirt is teeming with life when all its occupants are deflecting. Envision the many crowded city subways or streets you have ever attempted to sue in rush hour. That is a wander in a vacant wilderness in comparison with the multitudes of dirt dwellers living underneath your toes. Just one gram of dirt -- roughly the size of a navy bean -- retains 100 million to 1 billion germs, 100,000 to 1 million parasites, 1,000 to 1 billion algae, also 1,000 to 100,000 protozoa.

The dirt's microscopic multitudes share an area with more significant invertebrates, a lot of whom it is possible to view with the naked eye, like springtails, mites, and beetles. Populations of microscopic organisms and soil invertebrates produce a varied and highly working soil food web (see Chapter 3 for additional information). And they are the same fascinating animals that convert your lawn wastes and kitchen bits to use compost.

You Can Do It! Home Composting Made Easy

I delve deeper into more detail concerning cold and hot composting methods within this segment, however, if you are keen to begin, leap ahead to Chapter 4 to find basic guidelines for developing an easy, freestanding heap.

Protozoa: *small (but not simple) organisms. They are single-celled heterotrophic eukaryotes.*

Some like it's hot!

As germs start breaking down organic matter, they release heat as a portion of the action. Should you construct a heap with the ideal mixture of components, moisture, and atmosphere, it immediately reaches 120 degrees Fahrenheit (49 degrees Celsius) and high and might heat up to destroy weed seeds or seeds. It is referred to as sexy or thermophilic composting. Specialized germs called thermophiles (heat-lovers) endure those elevated temps and keep eating and reproducing before these conditions are no more favorable -- which is, as soon as your heap runs from water, food, and atmosphere.

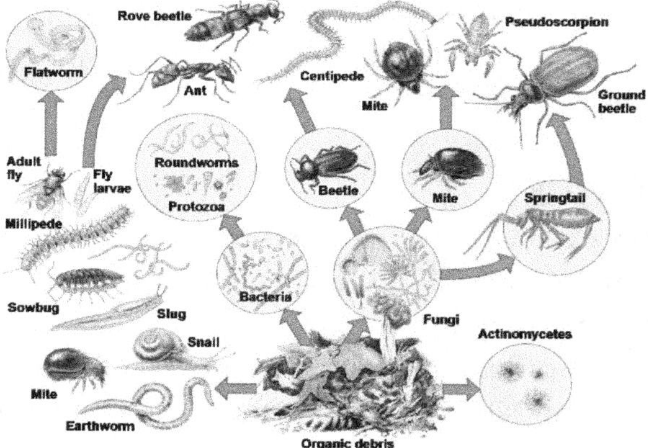

It's possible to deal with your property to keep relatively substantial temperatures by blending and remoistening (as required) before the favorite food sources have been depleted. Now, temperatures begin falling, and distinct microorganisms called mesophiles (which flourish in mild temperatures) happen over. Soil invertebrates also arrive if temperatures fall to combine in the decomposition procedure. Hot composting generates usable compost in as few as 3 or 4 months up to two or three weeks.

Cool clients

In slow or cold composting techniques, it might require 6 to 12 weeks or even more time to acquire usable mulch. Piles do not heat sufficiently to destroy weed seeds or seeds. On the other hand, the benefit is that the heap takes no maintenance on your character once you assemble it. Though you are not turning the heap to boost aeration or incorporating moisture, decomposer organisms may continue to crack the refuse. Mesophile and psychrophiles (cold-loving organisms) do the job at a lesser rate.

Vermicomposting (worm composting) and many types of sheet composting (dispersing organic material in addition to the ground to decompose in position) are deemed cold systems. Since they change from the conventional method of coping with a heap, these approaches have been covered in their chapters.

Reaping the Benefits of Composting

Composting saves you money and reduces global warming, helps you eliminate weight, and enhances your life! Overall, there might be a believer in this announcement, however, offered a choice between composting and merchandise infomercials blaring similar statements, I would go with composting as it

◊ Borrows money by cutting garbage collection prices and reducing, or eliminating, the need to purchase soil alterations, replacements, and fertilizers. You might even save your water bill because incorporating compost into your soil enhances its moisture-holding capacity.
◊ Reduces the quantity of methane (a greenhouse gas) generated when organic matter decomposes in landfills.
◊ Burns approximately 350 calories an hour because you flip the heap (for someone weighing 150 lbs).
◊ Might get you noticed by somebody who cares about among the preceding three things.

Still not sure? This segment offers more great reasons to carry up composting.

A much healthier, more successful garden

If you would like to develop a fantastic vegetable, flower, or herb garden, then begin with your own soil. Healthy, fertile soil means healthy, productive plants. And the very best thing you can do to make wholesome garden soil is to add compost. Here is what compost can do to the beds:

Add organic matter to improve soil structure and porosity: Soil consists of sand, silt, and clay particles. Soil structure refers to the structure of those particles -- the way they trap or clump together and create pore spaces that allow water and airflow through the ground. Soil porosity produces a healthful environment for plant roots to flourish. Adding compost helps soil retain moisture and nourishment so that you could be in a position to water and simmer less often. Adding compost also calms compacted clay dirt, reduces erosion, also boosts more significant drainage; thus, plant roots do not rot in moist soil.
Insert and nourish valuable soil microorganisms: Compost is chock full of beneficial microbes which add life to a garden dirt. If you add compost to the soil, the germs keep breaking down organic matter to release nourishment and also keep"bad" organisms in check.
Supply slow-release nourishment: Due to its nutrient content varies widely based upon the fundamental components and decomposition procedure, compost is known as a soil change, not just fertilizer. Nevertheless, compost includes vital plant nutrients and trace components to boost soil fertility. Additionally, mulch discharges its nutrients gradually while it decomposes farther on your own soil. Garden plants take advantage of the nutrients within an extended growing season. Most compound fertilizers release their nutrients at a fast burst; a number of their value might be missing if crops are not prepared to use it or even heavy rains or excess irrigation leach it off.

Silt : is granular material of a size between sand and clay, whose mineral origin is quartz

A much healthier community and planet

The numerous benefits of composting reach improving human gardens. Composting your yard waste and kitchen scraps in the home, instead of placing them out for garbage collection, provides you a path for part of the remedy for problems like overburdened landfills, pollution, and global warming. Listed below are a couple of reasons to divert your prized organic substances from going into the landfill:

◊ Composting extends the life of existing landfills and decreases the requirement to make others.
◊ Composting reduces transport costs and associated air pollutants from garbage hauling and collection.
◊ As organic waste decomposes in landfills, it creates acidic liquid (leachate) that can mix with other contaminants from the landfill and also seep into groundwater supplies.
◊ Organic waste, which is carefully compressed in landfills to decompose without oxygen, generates methane, which can be a greenhouse gas.
◊ Burning yard waste isn't a convenient option for refuge in metropolitan regions since it pollutes the atmosphere and exacerbates issues for individuals with allergies, asthma, bronchitis, and other respiratory difficulties. Burning waste can be prohibited in certain rural places; therefore, composting is an excellent alternate.
◊ A compost heap is a fantastic wildlife habitat that teems with invertebrates and leaves a snug house for valuable creatures like toads offering free pest management in your garden.

Leachate : *is any liquid that, in the course of passing through matter, extracts soluble or suspended solids*

2 TOOLS OF TRADE

If you are already gardening, then you likely can dive into composting together with resources you've got on hand. But if you are brand new to gardening and homemade, you are going to be delighted to hear you don't have to break your lender to make a tool arsenal.

This chapter indicates that the oversight of rotting organic matter necessitates just a few primary tools! A number of tools have titles that are appropriately used or disagree so that I allow you to sort out that. In addition, you get recommendations on characteristics to search for when buying quality gear, in addition to measures to take to maintain them in good shape. And since security should be the number one issue, the thing starts with a couple of fundamentals on staying safe and fit from the backyard.

Protacting Yourself in the components

Composting is enjoyable! You're able to keep it this way with a few straightforward steps: Wear gloves and other security equipment as necessary, and shield yourself from sunlight.

Obtaining a fantastic set of gloves

Many girls have a great deal of shoes in the cupboard. I have got a lot of garden gloves onto the shelf. I rarely pass a screen of art gloves without even needing to test them. Good-fitting, comfy gloves are crucial for your gardening and construction work. Should they don't"feel " in the middle of your job, you are very likely to pull them off, throw them apart (forgetting where they left them), and don't have any protection against scratches, scratches, and blisters. It's true that you can grab a cheap pair of cotton gloves in the hardware store or nursery to begin, but updating to better-quality gloves as soon as you find a set that suits you're rewarding. Producers have been combining helpful layout features with different substances to make a completely new batch of lettering styles that protect hands while providing much-needed flexibility and comfort. Here's a rundown of your options along with my suggestions:

Glove substances

◊ Goatskin comprising natural lanolin generates soft, cushioned leather, which matches just like, well, such as a glove.

◊ Wig handled through the immune system to become water-repellent and hand-washable guarantees the gloves do not become adobe brick because a few leather gloves do whenever they become wet in the backyard. Leather gloves also offer you some protection from thorns.

◊ Four-way extend nylon (the same material used for a whole lot of athletic equipment) fits easily through the rear of your hand.

Glove includes

◊ Padded palms provide comfort and gripping power when doing repetitive spinning and smelling errands.

◊ More extended wrists using a stretchy loop-and-tape closed to lock out dirt and also created taking off the gloves and yanking them back on fast and straightforward.

◊ Longer duration gloves (occasionally known as gauntlets) pay all or a portion of the forearm (most gloves complete in the wrist). This type is particularly helpful when dealing with plenty of thorny prunings.

◊ Reinforced palms include security and endurance.

◊ Waterproof helps maintain out water and heat in.

Shielding your eyes

If you chop mulch components -- with a handheld device or chipper/shredder machine -- always wear safety glasses or goggles to guard your eyes away from errant UFOs (unidentified flying organics). Ensure also to use these glasses when coping with heaps of narrow, long, or thorny stalks that might quickly whip back and hit you in your eye. Safety glasses also come in handy once you turn the hard organic thing that dissipates plenty of dust particles into the atmosphere. When allergies are an issue, safety eyeglasses (and a dust mask) can assist in preventing red, runny eyes along with other ailments. You may grab an affordable set of safety glasses in a hardware or home improvement store.

Shredder : a tool or machine that is used for cutting things into very small pieces

UFOs : unidentified flying object (mostquios, bugs, etc.)

Donning a dust mask

Based on the components on your mulch pile and in which you ship, turning organic things can stir up dust particles, pollen, or mold spores, which will be readily inhaled. Shredding leaves and leaves organic matter also generates beautiful pieces of drifting substance. In case you have asthma, allergies, or other respiratory problems, urge a dust mask to protect yourself through these laborious tasks. It is possible to buy cheap paper dust masks out of paint and hardware shops or search on the internet for several higher-quality options. For those who suffer from allergies or respiratory issues, these thoughts may help you enjoy your gardening tasks with fewer aerial issues:

◊　Sprinkle the mulch heap with water because you work to eliminate dust and debris.
◊　Refrain from turning heaps on windy days.
◊　Work outside after rain showers, due to humidity and rain disrupts the trip of windborne pollen.
◊　Restrict gardening tasks from the morning (5 to 10 a.m.), when the majority of pollen is discharged.
◊　Shower and change your clothing quickly after working at the backyard.

Blocking damaging rays with sunscreen and hat

If you are a northern-climate gardener, then you could be scratching your mind (or rolling your eyes) in my following suggestion. However, the sunlight's ultraviolet rays are harmful regardless of where you reside, and also skin cancer rates are upward around the world. Protect yourself by:

◊　Sporting a wide-brimmed hat
◊　Slathering on sunscreen with an SPF of 15
◊　Staying out of the sun from 10 a.m. to two pm, if the beams are most destructive
◊　Wearing long-sleeved tops and long trousers

Even if you believe you are only going from the mulch pile" for a moment," it is easy to become entangled (mulch is intriguing stuff), along with just two hours may sweep before you realize it. Please protect your self and remain hydrated with a great deal of drinking water!

Deciding on the ideal Tools and Equipment for Your Job

All you need to acquire composting is a long-handled fork, either a scoop or shovel and also a thing with which to chop up bigger stalks and prunings. However, like most occupations in the backyard, using the ideal tools for the job, which makes it a great deal simpler. This part guides you to choose tools that are perfect for your own home efforts. Tool descriptions can also mention other frequent gardening jobs they're developed because if you are searching for resources, this info might help you determine which styles offer you the best bang for the dollar.

Mixing things up using a pitchfork or mulch fork

You merely want one fork to begin composting, and since the qualities of different forks are much like I explain them collectively. Pitchforks and mulch forks possess five or four, slim, pliable, and also upward-curving tines created to effectively glide to a heap of organic substance, enabling you to hoist and toss into a new site. These forks are fantastic for moving massive clumps of tight, lightweight organic matter, like hay, straw, leaves, and plant trimmings. Use them to develop new compost piles and then flip them till the organic matter is rather decomposed. Then it is time to change into a shovel or dirt fork for turning almost-finished compost one final time moving finished mulch to your garden.

The principal differences between a pitchfork and a mulch fork would be the manage length and contour. Pitchfork grips are generally roughly 4 feet (1.2 meters) long with a direct finish. Compost fork grips are generally shorter -- approximately 3 ft (1 meter) long -- using a D-grip end. Additionally, pitchforks usually have thinner instrument heads compared to mulch forks.

Digging in using a dirt fork

Also called a digging fork or spading fork, that this instrument's flat prongs are thicker, shorter, and more durable than pitchfork or effluent fork tines. A dirt fork helps turn almost-finished mulch or dig hefty finished compost in a heap and integrating it in garden beds. Soil forks are also excellent tools for diving into compacted soil to loosen it if developing a new planting space. They are sometimes employed to break up clods and clumps of dirt and dig weedy patches, which makes it effortless to pull handfuls of weeds and even shake off the dirt off their origins. The briefer tines of dirt forks do not do the job in addition to pitchforks and mulch forks for transferring heaps of undecomposed organic matter; however, they do an adequate job of scooping up little piles of annuals or weeds pulled in the backyard.

Finding the lowdown on shovels and spades

The phrases"shovel" and also"spade" can be used interchangeably, as well as the language may vary by area too. Generally, however, a spade is a tool created for transferring substance, using a raised lip on every side of the blade to prevent pieces from falling away. A spade includes a sharp, right mind and can be used for digging. As previously explained by forks, a shovel may be used for altering substances both before and after that, but not so economically.

Rounded-blade shovel

A rounded-blade shovel functions as an all-purpose instrument for gardening tasks like turning almost-finished compost, pruning completed mulch out of a bin, including mulch into garden beds, also grinding openings into already-loose, sandy, or loamy soils.

Pointed-blade stinks

A pointed-blade spade has become the most versatile option quickly if you purchase just 1 grinding apply. It performs precisely the very same actions since the rounded blade shovel, while also permitting simpler grinding to compacted clay lands. The pointed knife helps chop up organic matter into smaller bits before tossing it in the compost pile, even though the square-blade spade, which I explain next, does a much better job for this undertaking. Even a pointed-blade spade is also valuable for cutting root spheres once dividing perennials.

Square-blade digging spade

Commonly used for pruning and pruning dirt in garden beds, even the more square-blade spade's shorter grip span and horizontal blade border also ease pruning up organic matter into pieces and pieces to get faster decomposition. (View other chopping options later in this chapter) The handle grips these brief, square-blade spades are smooth and straight, as they're on the curved - and - pointed-blade shovels, plus else they got a D-grip, that provides you additional gripping power because you wield the instrument for a chopper.
Purchase a shovel with a boost controller, and it's a thicker top border which enables your foot to shove against the blade using more electricity. This attribute is particularly beneficial if your backyard where lands are tough, rugged, or compressed.

Purchasing a high-quality hose

Straightforward accessibility to water is crucial because moisture is a vital element of a successful masonry attempt, and you'll likely need to moisten the natural thing periodically to maintain it decomposing correctly. A inexpensive hose will irritate you, kinking, breaking, and denying to spiral readily until you eventually give up and purchase a much better one. Splurge on a top-notch hose in the beginning and include a nozzle that lets you turn the stream on and off to save water at the same time you operate, besides, to fix the preferences for various watering activities in the backyard. For instance, a beautiful spray works well to gently moisturize everything without squandering water as possible work. **Nozzles** can be found in a vast selection of styles and costs.

You're able to purchase hoses or without pliers, however to your first hose that a reel is strongly suggested. It allows you to coil and also keep your hose fast, readily, and, and besides, it extends the life span of the nozzle. Pick out of free-standing or wall-mounted reels; a few retract automatically while some must be wound.

It is possible to prolong the life of the hose using these easy guidelines:

◊   Do not abandon a hose lying from sunlight.
◊   Drain a hose until winter sets in, and keep it inside throughout the off-season.
◊   Do not drag a nozzle over rugged surfaces.
◊   Coil a nozzle when not in use.

Water pressure diminishes since the hose becomes more, so buy a hose that's just provided that you want.

Nozzles : short tube with a taper or constriction used (as on a hose) to speed up or direct a flow of fluid

Transferring compost in buckets or tarps

Compost transfer around the backyard can be thrifty and low-tech because of a heavy-duty plastic contractor's window (not a lightweight family one) or even a tarp. A bucket is excellent for moving small amounts of compost. As for more enormous heaps, it takes some time and labor to move a lot of compost with only two or 2. However, think of all of the superb free exercise you will receive.

Have a look at a garden supply shop for hardy tarps or carry luggage with reinforced corner grips that permit you to collect the corners and then drag the package on your own or take it between 2 individuals. Another option is that a contractor-grade polyethylene tarp with reinforced grommets in the corners. They may include their grips, or you can slide nylon rope or spans of fabric through the grommets to create your own. Polyethylene tarps are watertight and tear-resistant.

Tarps will also be ideal for projecting over compost piles to keep moisture in humid climates and protect against excessive moisture out of turning your mulch to a soggy mess in moist climates. Additionally, covering a recently assembled stack with a tarp helps keep heat as the decomposition process will get underway. Polyethylene functions better as a refuge; however, burlap is much far better than nothing!

Hauling mulch with wheelbarrows or lawn carts

If you create a good deal of mulch and also have a massive yard with a great deal of planting and plant places to haul your beautiful mulch into, a wheelbarrow or garden cart is an asset. They are available in some versions, sizes, and weights.

Many wheelbarrows have a single bicycle positioned ahead, and when you lift the rear end off the floor to push it together. (Even though two-wheeler wheelbarrows can also be accessible, they are generally construction-grade to support substantial loads. You still need to lift and drive) Wheelbarrows are somewhat less secure compared to garden carts, however more maneuverable in tight spaces. Based upon their weight and of these substances inside, dumping out everything by leaning the wheelbarrow on the conclusion is rather straightforward.

When you have noticed one wheelbarrow, you have pretty much seen them; however, backyard carts offer you a wide assortment of styles. Carts disperse the weight of their load within two and four wheels, which makes them more comfortable to restrain compared to wheelbarrows. Carts may be pulled or pushed, and a few could be hammered by yard tractors as well as bikes if you are so inclined.

Their usually rectangular or boxy shape does not allow the same maneuverability for backing up and turning round in tight quarters because wheelbarrows do. Some garden carts seem like crossbreeds using wheelbarrows but possess deeper beds and broader wheel systems for equilibrium. Some carts could be raised and lifted like wheelbarrows; many others have panels that turn up or could be removed entirely for ease in loading and unloading. Other fashions fold for storage throughout the off-season.

These questions can help you find the best option for your requirements when buying either a wheelbarrow or garden cart:

◊ Just how much weight and quantity can it hold?
◊ Just how much weight could you push or pull?
◊ Can its measurements travel readily through regions in your lawn, like between garden rows or to the tight corner in which the compost bins have been?
◊ How hardy are the brakes? Can they encourage a substantial load without falling? Start looking for tires if you will need traction.
◊ What's the building material? Can it hold up on your climate?
◊ Are the grips comfy to grip?
◊ Are metal components rust-resistant?

Additional Tools and Gadgets to your Enthusiastic Composter

Compost can create itself without the assistance of any gadgets, but if you would like to speed up things a little or simply get close and personal with the pile, have a look at the extra instruments and gadgets covered within this part.

Analyzing your mulch's temperature

I am not even for gadgets, but I do adore my toaster thermometer. Mounted at the end of a very long probe (approximately 20 inches, or 0.5 meters), this thermometer is perfect for sticking to the middle of a heap to track its temperature.

Aerating your mulch

The very best way of integrating more air in your compost would be to turn the heap entirely. But if you do not have enough time or disposition to flip it, then an aerating tool could possibly be helpful. An aerating twist also called a mulch twist that functions on the principle which it is simpler to dip a lengthy implement deep inside the organic thing to poke round -- particularly within the limits of a little and thin bin -- it would be to stir up things from over using a pitchfork or shovel. Cranks function like giant corkscrews.

You stick the instrument in addition to the mulch, then turn the deal to run it through the natural thing, then pull it out or drizzle it by simply turning the handle from the opposite way.

While looking for composting gear, you might come across an aerating tool that somewhat simplifies a harpoon. Paddles lie flush using the instrument as you dip it via the natural issue. As you pull on back the tool outside, the paddles pop to the sides to grab and proceed organic issue. The harpoon aerators I have tried need more physical exertion than a mulch twist, along with the paddles that have gotten stuck in high tech or sterile material, which makes the instrument troublesome to extract. If you are an enormous burly weightlifter, pulling a stuck aerating tool might be no consequence! But if you are puny (such as me) or have shoulder or back issues, that the harpoon style might not match you.

Bear in mind, based on where you reside, and your pile is quite likely to be home to all types of animals, from frogs and toads into hedgehogs, especially in winter. Stirring your pile might upset or even kill them.

Contemplating pruning tools

You do not need monitoring tools to be a great composter. As I explained earlier in the chapter, both pointed- and - square-blade shovels can block weeds and plant substance. As you lean crops, you may use pruners and loppers for decreasing organic matter into smaller bits. But in case you have a lot of organic matter to slice and dice, other instrument options incorporate a machete or a cutter mattock Machetes and filler mattocks are sharp resources that can lead to significant harm; therefore caution is necessary.

◊ Machete: You have probably seen a celebrity in a film whacking through thick jungle foliage using a machete. This long-bladed knife works good for chopping up backyard refuse. Sizes vary, however a machete blade is generally about 15 to 20 inches (38 to 51 centimeters), and a 5- to 6-inch (12- to 15-centimeter) manage. You will need a flat, secure chopping surface to put the substance on for chopping. I understand a gardener that laps an older tree stump. As opposed to paying someone to grind the stump outside, she will have chipped off nearly all of it himself within a couple of decades.

◊ Cutter mattock: A cutter mattock includes a cutting edge blade like a little strand, which works nicely for a natural thing. Its next blade is ordinarily an adz blade, used for grinding in hard dirt or hoeing. Mattock tool heads weigh from 3 to 2 lbs (1.5 to 3 kilograms) and manage approximately 3 to 4 feet (1 to 1.2 meters) long.

Tool-Buying Tips

A technical tool appears to be accessible for pretty much every single garden job. If your present impulse would be to simplify somewhat in line with the garage with more gadgets, then carefully think about what sorts of gardening activities that you perform on a standard basis. Then buy top-notch tools to assist people chores go easily. The subsequent sections deal with questions to ask when assessing a specific tool.

How can this feel?

A tool functions best when it is comfortable for you to work with, and only you are able to make that decision making. Head into the shop, remove the instrument from its bin or hook, and heft it. Can the weight and equilibrium feel right? Is the length appropriate? Since many gardening tasks are repetitive, utilizing resources that are too bulky or uncomfortable whatsoever induces muscle strain, therefore if a tool does not feel right, do not purchase it. There is great diversity in the software marketplace nowadays, so spend some opportunity to choose a top-notch tool that feels excellent to you.

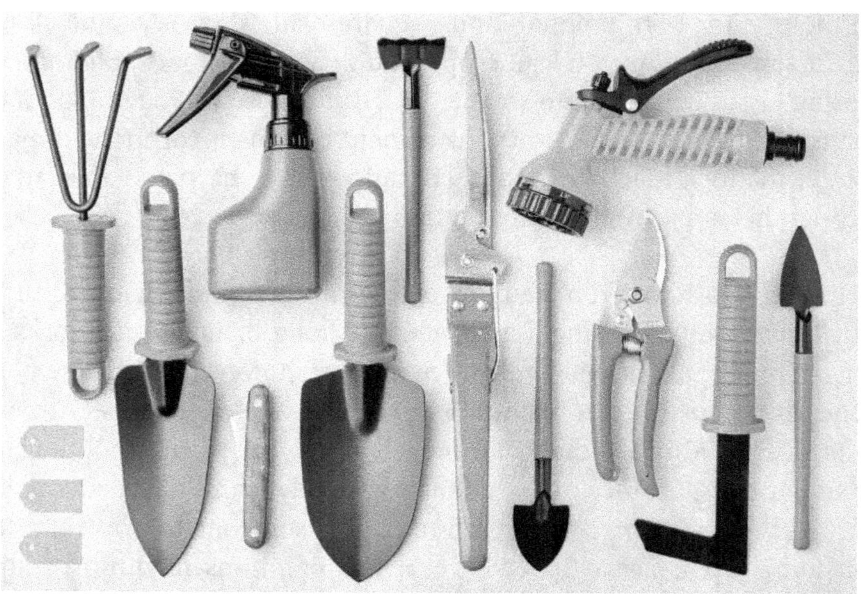

How is it made?

For long-lasting and robust durability, pick tools that possess the blade (the instrument head) along with the collar (the way where the blade attaches to the grip) forged in 1 piece of metal. Forged tools are thicker and more potent than tools that are stamped (substantially cut and flexed) out of a sheet of metal. Even less costly, stamped tools are somewhat poorer and not as durable. High-carbon forged steel is sturdy and lets you keep a sharp sword as time passes. Stainless steel tools can also be great and give the extra plus of rust resistance. But, it is somewhat more challenging to maintain a sharp edge on stainless steel compared to carbon dioxide. Aluminum typically isn't hardy enough for the long haul, but although current inventions like magnesium and aluminum metal provide durability with less total weight Materials-wise, many management options are either fiberglass or wood. Ash and hickory are the most potent hardwoods for instrument handles. But, fiberglass handles are more durable and last longer. If you are thinking about keeping tools or returning to the tool shed in the conclusion of the afternoon, fiberglass might be a more significant investment in the long term. Evaluate the differences:

Hardwood tool handles
◊ Are less costly than fiberglass
◊ Absorb the shock of repetitive moves (like dig, lift, throw, dig, lift, throw) to lessen muscular fatigue
◊ Require seasonal upkeep to stop splitting
◊ Can be trimmed to size for a more comfortable fit

Fiberglass tool handles
◊ are somewhat costlier than hardwood
◊ Our lightweight, but do not absorb the shock of repetitive movements
◊ Are maintenance-free
◊ Sport bright-colored handles which are easy to put from the backyard

Showing Your Tools Many TLC

The easy step of cleaning gear after every use helps maintain them free from rust and also in great shape to function for you -- instead of against you -- for many decades to come. (Something is gratifying about departure Grandma's or Grandpa's applications on to another generation.)

Giving everything a Fast cleaning

Set up a straightforward cleaning bucket in which you save your resources. With everything near at hand, tidying your resources requires only a moment or two. All you will need are rags for wiping dirt grime and employing sandpaper, a stiff brush for scratching off mud, along with a rust-inhibiting instrument lubricant to wash metal components using a rag after cleansing the instrument.

Maintaining wooden grips

Wood may crack, split, or create splinters if moisture works in. Wipe manages tender after use and keep your tools from harm's way from sunlight, rain, wind, and snow. At the conclusion of the gardening year, liven up the deal. Utilize a fine-grit glue to remove splinters. Seal the wood from moisture from stripping it down with a cone dipped in boiled linseed oil, which can be found at hardware and home-and-garden shops. Apply multiple coats within a couple of days to enable the oil to penetrate. This practice may also marginally rejuvenate an older deal and maintain the instrument working more (a particularly useful hint if you discover a deal in a yard or rummage sale).

3 THE DECOMPOSITION PROCESS

Your compost heap is a portion of food online, comprising classes of ever-larger inhabitants swallowing plant material along with each other. Collectively, they choose the kitchen scraps and compost along with other substances and change it to attractively rich growing substance. Within this chapter describe (in not-too-scientific phrases) both significant procedures -- physical and chemical -- which split big chunks of uncooked organic matter into smaller and smaller parts, which are finally utilized to fuel more significant cycles of existence.

Additionally, you get descriptions of the significant decomposer organisms on your mulch pile. I know that studying "bugs" is not everybody's preferred cup of java, but I am prepared to wager you'll get hooked on new creatures later or sooner.

In the meantime, you do not need to know whc's doing everything to handle a thriving mulch system on your garden. You merely understand how to maintain the decomposers working out. The final major part of the chapter provides recommendations on handling water, food, atmosphere, and heat to maintain your property celebrities performing at peak ability.

Decomp 101: The Way Rotting Works

Composting creatures use one of two standard procedures of decomposition to break all the debris on your compost heap -- physical or chemical. The procedures of physical and chemical decomposition are explained in these sections. In addition, I explain how these composters socialize on your mulch community.

Moving to bits: The bodily split

Soil invertebrates (animals lacking backbones) are still an incredibly diverse community billed with the endless job of reducing mountains of natural refuse to smaller and smaller pieces. Based on species, they also assault their work using mouthparts designed for biting, chewing, rasping, shredding, or even milling plant issues.

25

These diverse chomping efforts decrease more significant bits of organic matter into smaller ones using much more surface space, which subsequently allows bacteria and other compound decomposers (that I explain in the following section) to acquire a foothold and operate more efficiently.

Physical decomposers behave in the first phases of your mulch pile, however as bacterial action warms up along with the temperatures increase, they leave (or perish). When temperatures fall, you will see all kinds of movement and life as organic decomposers return into the heap to keep their job.

Freeing the enzymes: The compound breakdown

Throughout your mulch heap's procedure for chemical decomposition, germs like bacteria and parasites release enzymes that break down complex organic compounds into simpler compounds, which decomposers can subsequently absorb in their bodies as nourishment. Other organisms get nourishment by eating the germs. And as germs die, the chemicals tied up into their bodies have been published and be available for one more production of organisms to utilize.

However, efficiently they operate, germs and other decomposers finally reach a stage where some chemicals can not be broken down any farther. These compounds of decomposition become connected to form humus, which desirable, crumbly, dark brownish result of composting. (Jump back to 1 to learn more about valuable humus.)

Maintaining equilibrium throughout the food net

The connections between members of the mulch pile community are not always favorable; however, the cows -- from all of their eating and being consumed -- contribute to providing you excellent compost. A food series depicts what every living organism eats to receive nutrients and energy, and subsequently, that eats it. The very first connection is a plant that's absorbed by the next connection in the series, possibly a grasshopper, who's subsequently eaten by means of a quail, etc. A food net depicts a broader community of organisms engaging in several food chains that are distinct. Your mulch pile acts as a food net, encouraging diverse life forms and countless people in their continuing venture of breaking and recycling organic things. These varied organisms produce a high working food internet by:

◊ Eating, digesting, and beneficial nutrition in forms which other organisms could consume

◊ Regulating populations of organisms thus no special group burgeons from control

◊ Getting food themselves to get higher-level customers in the food web

Your compost heap's food net always starts with essential residue -- leaves, grass clippings, manure, coffee grounds, kitchen scraps, and so forth. All that"crap" you pile up provides life to primary decomposers, that would be the very first to sit at the dining table. They include both physiological decomposers and compound decomposers.

Next are secondary customers, organisms which eat primary customers. Some of them you can spy together with the naked eye, like beetles and springtails. Others are still microscopic, such as protozoa that consume bacteria.

Tertiary customers eat leading customers. All these are the more significant (comparatively speaking) residents of your mulch pile, like centipedes and beetles, which you may readily see scurrying away once you flip past a mound of organic matter employing your fork or spade.

Who Is Doing the Hard Work?

I used to have a rest from tossing still another heap of organic matter from 1 bin to another to lean in my pitchfork, wipe my sweaty forehead, examine my achievements, and believe (slightly virtuously) I had been"composting." Then I had the fantastic chance to choose a Master Composter class and discovered that I could not lay claim to this effort.

Though I had been supplying the ideal conditions for these, it was billions and billions (and much more billions) of decomposer organisms that have been"composting" in my behalf. I don't mind playing second fiddle for this intriguing cast of characters. They perform their roles to perfection when I nudge them together only a bit, and then continue to carry out much if I ignore their demands completely.

In the subsequent sections, you receive a quick introduction into the creatures on the job on your mulch pile. I talk the compound decomposers original -- since they do the majority of the work and then present the bodily decomposers.

(For more about the distinction between chemical and physical decomposition, see the prior section"Decomp 101: The Way Exactly To Works.") In addition, I throw in some"Interesting facts" across the way: Understanding these pieces of trivia will not make you some more productive at home, but they might provide you the advantage you will need to make it large on Jeopardy! in case you ought to aspire thus.

Counting on compound decomposers

The particular microbes involved with compound decomposition -- bacteria, actinomycetes, fungi, and protozoa -- will be the topic of the upcoming sections. I explain to them in the general arrangement of the population figures in a conscious composting attempt.

Bacteria develop the heating

Compounds are parasitic organisms. They are the most many chemical decomposers, including 80 to 90% of those microbes functioning on your heap. They hitch a trip into the compost celebration on your primary ingredients; therefore, the kinds and amounts of bacteria change with every pile you assemble. The greater variety in your components, the greater variety of your decomposers, and finally, your final compost is going to have more nutrition and valuable characteristics.

Different germs thrive at various temperature ranges. When temperatures rise or fall, judgment inhabitants die or be inactive as well as also other species carry over to restrain the activity. As bacterial inhabitants flourish -- eating, reproducing, and dying -- that they give off heat for a by-product. You may read more about handling the warmth to make the most of your composting attempts later in this chapter in the section"Tuning the warmth."

Interesting fact: One production of bacteria on your mulch pile lives just 20 to half an hour. Kinda gives new meaning to the expression, "So much to do, and little time!"

More germs: Actinomycetes get in the act

As previously bacteria inhabitants consume all of the easy-to-break-down chemicals, including simple sugars, actinomycetes (a-tin-oh-mahyseet-EEZ) take more to operate on complicated organic materials like bark and fibrous or woody stalks.

Actinomycetes are naturally-occurring germs, though they shape long, branching threads or filaments which look similar to bacterial structures compared to germs. Contrary to other varieties of germs on your mulch, you can see stains of actinomycetes using the naked eye only because they form pre-assembled strands that resemble cobwebs dispersing throughout the outer to 6 inches (10 to 15 centimeters) of a heap.

Interesting fact: The compost's pleasant earthy odor is generated by actinomycetes discharging gases throughout the decomposition procedure.

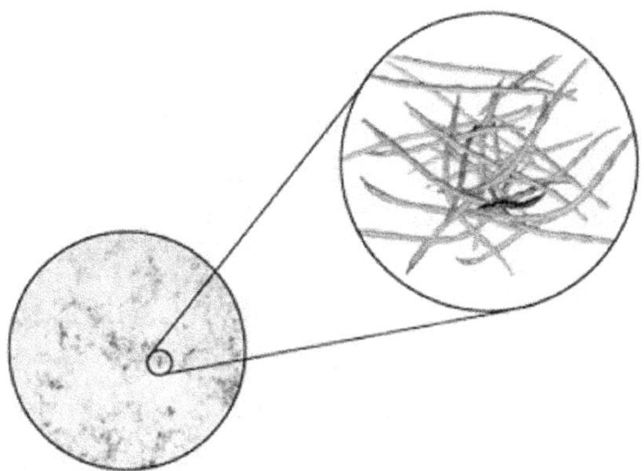

Fungi Affect the procedure

Such as actinomycetes, fungi on your mulch pile break down demanding organic things that previous rounds of decomposers leave, like dried, dried, or high-carbon substances. Most pollutants require less oxygen than germs do; therefore, pollutants are essential decomposers in heaps of high-carbon substances, like wood chips or sawdust (see"Rationing that the carbons and nitrogens" later in this chapter).

Lots of distinct parasite types exist on your heap, such as microscopic species, in addition to vague, fuzzy, whitish colonies. In the event you've rotting wood on your heap, you might even find mushrooms sprouting, as mushrooms insure dropped tree trunks decomposing to a forest floor!

Interesting fact: The yeast that is used to consume bread is, in fact, a kind of fungi!

Protozoa play together (the type of)

Such as bacteria, protozoa are microscopic, one-celled organisms that look as secondary and primary customers in your mulch. Protozoan inhabitants are much less critical in quantity -- and consequently effectiveness -- on your mulch pile compared to formerly described compound decomposers.

New truth: Protozoa are apparent and become an identical color as what they have just eaten.

Profiting from bodily decomposers

A lot of the bodily decomposers, like beetles and millipedes, are big enough to readily spot from over. Others, like mites and springtails, are miniature, but still observable with the naked eye if you scoop up a couple of compost and peer-reviewed closely. Surprisingly perhaps, the most significant population of physical decomposers -- even nematodes, or roundworms -- are still nearly all microscopic therefore you likely won't find them. (But in case you get lucky and detect something which looks like a shifting strand of human hair, then you are probably observing a nematode.)

I will head out on a limb and admit if you are reading this novel, you are not a dirt invertebrate like such other bodily decomposers. But should you chop or split organic matter into smaller portions before blending it into your heap, then you can add on to the list of physical decomposers I explain next.

Nematodes (roundworms)

On Your mulch pile, nematodes, also known as roundworms, are allies on your attempt to recycle organic matter and nutrients. They eat decaying plant material and also eat different decomposers, like bacteria and parasites.

Tens of tens of thousands of nematode species exist globally in every kind of surroundings; there are numerous that scientists have not come close to discovering them. Based on species, nematodes are technical eaters, absorbing organic matter, bacteria, fungi, protozoa, as well as their damaging (in the human standpoint) nematode cousins. (See the previous section"Counting on compound decomposers" to learn more about bacteria and other germs.)

Interesting fact: Nematodes can move through the soil just when a picture of moisture encircles soil particles. During dry conditions or flooding, nematodes go dormant, reviving when soil moisture is available.

Mites

Mites belong to this category of creatures called arachnids, identified as a part with four pairs of legs and no antennae. Much like nematodes, the world is covered with plentiful lava species using varying perform agendas. Even though some mites are

Nematodes : *any unsegmented worm of the phylum Nematoda, having an elongated, cylindrical body.*

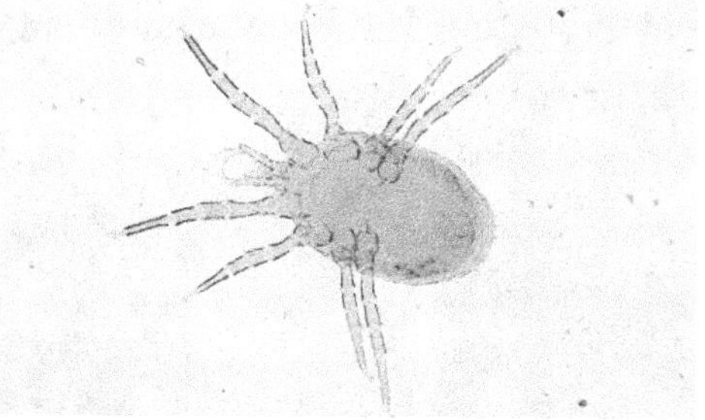

noteworthy garden bugs (spider mites), several valuable pests help degrade organic thing on your mulch pile. For example, mold spores (also referred to as fermentation mites) feed chiefly on yeasts in debris. Predatory mites in compost consume diverse insects and insect eggs.

Interesting fact the majority of mold spores have transparent bodies.

Springtails

These fascinating small wingless insects quantify out of 1/16 inch (1.6 millimeters) around 1/4 inch (6.3 millimeters) in length. They've a hinged, tail-like appendage that goes forwards underneath the gut and can be held in place from the stomach with a"latch." Since the latch is released, the appendage" springs" down and slides the insect to the atmosphere, such as a pogo stick. (It is true. I am not sufficiently inventive to make up that.)

Due to the leaping movement, springtails are occasionally confused for insects, but they have not one of these pests' problem traits like biting or spreading disorder. Sometimes, some springtail species could chew on roots or leaves of tender tails, although harm is generally insignificant. Established plants aren't at any risk from springtails.

Take any springtails you detect as more valuable residents of your mulch pile, chewing decomposing plant matter, blossoms, viruses, bacteria, pollen, algae, as well as insect urine. Since air and moisture pass easily through their body surfaces, springtails are exceptionally vulnerable to drying out. Therefore, you are going to probably spy them at the moister environs of the mulch pile.

New truth: Springtails"spring" 3 to 4 inches (7.6 to ten centimeters) at one jump.

Sowbugs and pillbugs

Quite similar in look, those pesky crustaceans breathe with gills, therefore that they need living accommodations that provide moisture and higher humidity. You will probably discover sowbugs or pillbugs (occasionally referred to as woodlice) in moist regions towards the middle or bottom of this mulch heap where they feed on decaying plant matter. Even though they're not annoying enough to be tagged as insects, sowbugs and pillbugs can feed tender living plant cells, for example, young seedlings growing in moist, organically fertile soil.

Adults develop around 3/8-inch (9.5-millimeters) extended and possessed different, round body sections and seven pairs of arms. Sowbugs have "taillike" appendages; pillbugs do not. Witl no tails to get in the way, pillbug roster into tight balls should the are feeling threatened, which clari fies another common name appre ciated by children: "roly-poly."

New truth: Sowbugs and pillbug are linked to crayfish, lobster, and shrimp.

Millipedes and centipedes

At first, millipedes and centipedes seem similar since they have many body sections and segments; however, there are lots of distinctions. Millipedes feed on damp decaying plant matter, helping divide the contents of your mulch pile. But, centipedes feed only on living animals, particularly insects and insect larvae. They kill their prey by copying them injecting venom. Centipedes can employ your compost heap for a hunting ground.

It is generally far better to depart millipedes or centipedes concealed on your mulch pile, but should you decide to pick up them, wear protective gloves and safety glasses. Centipede bites may be painful, though they're not generally life-threatening unless the sufferer has allergic responses or is a little kid.

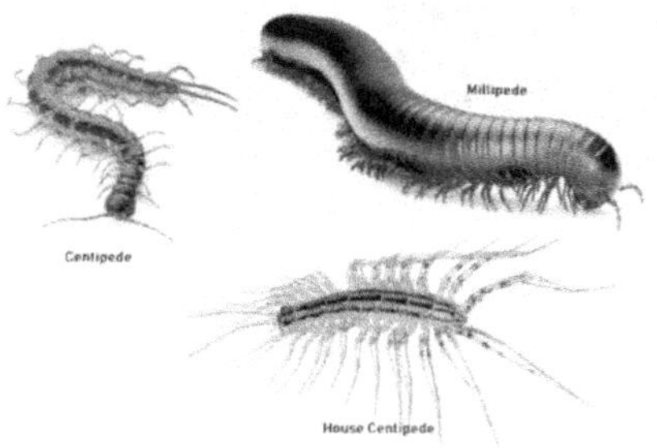

In these instances, seek advice from your doctor or poison control center immediately. Millipedes can dislodge an irritating fluid, which leaves a foul odor, which causes skin responses, and might be damaging if it gets to your eyes.

Some species may start this material a few inches!
Interesting fact: Despite their titles, millipedes do not fit a million thighs, nor do centipedes wander about on 100. A more inclined leg count is significantly less than 100 to get millipedes and approximately 30 to get centipedes.

Beetles

Beetles are all hard-shelled pests with two sets of wings tucked from their spine. Numerous beetle species function during your compost pile, either throughout their larval life period (if they are called grubs) and as adult beetles. Grubs feed on rotting organic matter. Beetles may have organic matter but also seek out prey like fly larvae (maggots), mites, and nematodes.
Interesting fact: Different beetle species are beneficial mulch dwellers since they consume the gardener's nemeses -- snails and slugs.

Snails and slugs

Snails have protective outside coil cubes; slugs are all soft-bodied. Otherwise, they display similar features, including the unfortunate capacity to decimate your vegetable or vegetable overnight. Should you reside in humid or wet climates with mild winters in which snails and slug inhabitants are widespread, you are bound to encounter them seeking new plant debris on your mulch pile. You might opt to ruin them as if they or their eggs still live in the final compost once you distribute it on your backyard, you have only given them a free pass into the mind of the buffet.

New truth: Snails and slugs emerge during the night, slipping along the floor and other surfaces using a full muscular"foot" that leaves supporting a mucous trail. If you do not observe these silvery slime trails, you have to monitor another offender to blame for almost any plant destruction.

Ants

The majority of the physical decomposers on your mulch desire moist conditions to endure, but rodents move into create nests only if circumstances are slightly dry. They will depart if you thoroughly moisten the heap and cook this up to elevated temperatures.
Abundant ant action is an indication your organic thing is dry for quick decomposition, which might or may not issue for you.

Many rodents are valuable at a mulch pile, eating all sorts of stuff, such as parasites, food seeds, and even other insects. They also help create a more abundant compost by distributing essential minerals like potassium and phosphorous from 1 place into another.

New truth: Ants can lift 20 times their weight loss.

Flies

Flies are two-winged pests which are rarely problematic using a mulch pile. Adult flies feed on organic material and deposit their eggs compost piles to supply a ready food supply of hatching larvae (maggots). Maggots, consequently, are consumed by fleas and other animals, so it is all part of the food web.

In case maggot inhabitants seem out-of-control (or gross you out), heat your heap -- large fever ranges kill fly larvae.

Should you encounter issues with bugs that are airborne, like houseflies or horseflies, buzzing about your compost heap, then eliminate your pitchfork, as your heap needs care. Properly tended compost does not attract flies. New truth: Flies are thought to transport over 1,941,000 distinct types of germs, some of which are going to wind up on your mulch pile to break down organic matter.

Earthworms

Earthworms will be the most significant homemade machines, swallowing and digesting organic things to deposit their abundant waste, known as casts or castings. Earthworms are essential to this world's recycling of organic matter and soil construction, in addition to your composting attempts, they deserve their own chapter.

Interesting fact: Even though worms don't have any eyes, they could feel light.

Developing a Productive Work Environment

Preceding sections within this chapter give a review of the most significant players on your mulch pile. It's interesting things to understand, but you do not have to memorize the titles of organisms to assist them operate effectively. Simply produce and keep a hospitable living environment for them. Their demands for life are very similar to mine and yours: water, food, atmosphere, and proper temperature. The rest of the chapter describes the perfect method to supply continuing life service to your composting creatures.

Rationing that the carbons and nitrogens

All organic thing you enhance your compost pile includes nitrogen and carbon in its own cells.

Many decomposers guzzling organic thing on your mulch pile favor a diet which comprises 30 times as much carbon as nitrogen (C:N), or 30:1. They utilize carbon-rich substances for energy and also nitrogen-rich substance for cells. The nearer you come to blending which perfect ratio along with your components, the more effectively the organisms can use it, and the quicker you get useable compost.

When there's more carbon than nitrogen (for example, cardboard includes a ratio of 600:1), a lot of generations of organisms have to lean through that carbon, then die to free the nitrogen in their bodies to its next generation of decomposers to utilize, and so forth. The composting process remains as the restricted nitrogen is poisonous, but it would happen much quicker if the components' ratios were nearer to 30:1 in the beginning.

An excessive amount of carbon slows down things, but also much nitrogen has its very own unpleasant impact. In case you have, for example, a pile of grass clippings 25:1 with no carbons to blend with this, odor issues aren't far behind. Since decomposers do not have a carbon to decide on all that nitrogen since they operate, surplus nitrogen is lost into the air since damaging ammonia gas.

To put it differently, three packs filled with brown stuff combined with one cart filled with green things. Another option is a 50-50 mixture of brown. Do not get bogged down in numbers; composting will nonetheless occur at distinct ratios, and thus don't be worried about precision. With time, you are going to create combinations of components that work well for you.

Sizing particles down

Step-by-step directions on creating a first mulch pile, I suggest chopping up many ingredients into little pieces. I also mention that you don't require whole uniformity with just little pieces because some bigger chunks improve aeration. Remember that for Nearly All the components, the bigger the bits of an organic thing, the quicker the speed of decomposition since:

◊ Plant materials' defense mechanisms against intrusion by microbes are reduced by scratches, cuts, and wounds out of chopping and shredding.
◊ The greater surface area has been made with lots and many little pieces. Higher surface area allows physical and chemical decomposers to more paths of attack.
◊ When constructing your heap, smaller, uniform bits with plenty of surface space are simpler to moisten thoroughly.
◊ Uniform substances are more comfortable to flip and remoisten.
◊ Uniform materials self-insulate and heating up quickly to make a sexy heap (more on this coming up in"Tuning the warmth").

How small is small ? Reduce the majority of your organic thing to 2-inch-long (5-centimeter) pieces and bits.

Handling moisture and atmosphere

Pollutants and aeration are usually discussed as separate issues in your mind; however, I find it is helpful to think about them together as your activities to control water and atmosphere in the compost heap are tightly connected. Billions of pore spaces encircle the particles on your own compost. Pores allow water and air to circulate throughout the compost components. When there's inadequate moisture, then the decomposer organisms shut up shop. On the flip side, if pores have been bombarded with oxygen, water is slowed, and you are stuck using a musty anaerobic (without air) compost heap to manage. Your intention is to balance air, and moisture amounts to maximize conditions for your decomposers, thus optimizing your composting attempts. Here is what you want to understand.

Maintaining sufficient moisture

The organisms that I explained earlier in this chapter need moisture to live. The majority of them play their decomposing magical in ultrathin films of water onto the face of natural particles. If your heap moisture level drops under 35 to 40 percent and stuff dried out, the majority of the monsters die or go dormant.

The perfect moisture content to your mulch heap is 40 to 60%. Nope, there is no requirement to consider anything! A simple procedure to gauge moisture content would be to squeeze several handfuls of substances from other regions of the heap. Everything needs

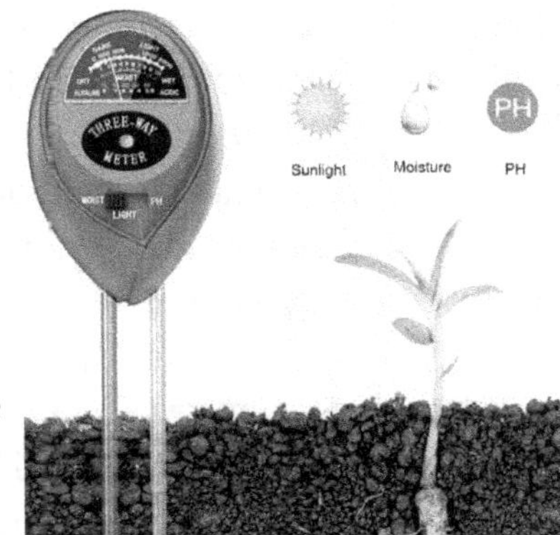

to feel moist, such as a wrung-out sponge. If it does not, it is time to add water.

It's possible to help preserve present moisture on your open compost heap by covering it with a tarp.

Having too much of a great thing: Drowning air out

On the opposite hand, soggy materials disability your home. Moisture content over 65 to 70 percent cubes air stream and develops to stinky circulatory conditions. Nutrients also leach from excessively wet mulch piles. If it's possible to squeeze over just a drop or 2 of water from a couple of components, the heap is too moist.

Pore distances at the heap provide essential oxygen to its survival of composting creatures. Pores also allow for the flow of carbon dioxide, which can be a by-product of the decomposing efforts. Adequate aeration helps preserve high temperatures, which create quicker speeds of decomposition and destroy weed seeds and seeds. (Pile temperatures have been coated in an upcoming part)

If you reside in exceptionally moist areas, covering your heap helps stop it from turning rancid through a deluge.

Locating the best equilibrium

Fine-tune your heap's moisture and atmosphere amounts from:

◊   Minding the organic thing to introduce additional air or dry out wet stuff. A correctly aerated pile does not have any undesirable smells. If it smells, it is probably too wet and has to be turned!

◊   Including abrasive carbon substances, such as leaves, straw, or sawdust, to soak up excess moisture.

◊   Rewetting materials should they wash out, typically in the same moment you flip the heap.

Tuning the temperature

Many decomposing activities on your mulch pile occurs in just two temperatures ranges -- mesophilic and thermophilic -- using various organisms thriving in every.

Mesophilic creatures operate from approximately 40 to 104 degrees Fahrenheit (4 to 40 degrees Celsius), even though they're most effective on your mulch pile from 70 to 90 degrees Fahrenheit (21 to 32 degrees Celsius). Mesophilic bacteria get active originally on the easy-to-decompose substances, including natural sugars. They create heat for a by-product of the hectic consumption, reproducing, and dying, which induces your mulch pile's temperature to grow. Not able to run at higher temperatures, so the mesophiles are usurped by thermophiles.

Thermophilic creatures flourish in 105 to 140 degrees Fahrenheit (41 to 60 degrees Celsius), though some can operate around 175 degrees Fahrenheit (79 degrees Celsius). In this sexy stage, these heat-tolerant germs begin breaking down the challenging stuff, including complex carbohydrates.

Recognizing a thermophilic compost heap

Although generally labeled since the thermophilic composting method (or even"hot" composting), this procedure also comprises two stages of mesophilic decomposition that sandwich the center hot stage.

1. Stage 1: Mesophilic (moderate temperature) germs and soil invertebrates begin the procedure. The first temperature ranges at a compost pile differ based on its components, total dimensions, moisture, and aeration, in addition to your geographical region. As a general principle, a well-constructed heap's first temperature runs approximately 50 to 70 degrees Fahrenheit (10 to 21 degrees Celsius) and increases rapidly in one to 5 times. Mesophilic decomposers predominate around 104 degrees Fahrenheit (40 degrees Celsius). The longer perfect your mixture of carbon to sulfur components, particle size, humidity, and atmosphere (see previous sections for more about those elements), the quicker your stack will warm, sometimes within hours.

2. Stage 2: Thermophilic (high fever) germs take at 105 degrees Fahrenheit (41 degrees Celsius). Based upon precisely the same heap features listed in Stage 1, besides, to further turning to boost aeration and remoistening as required, temperatures leap fast into 120 degrees Fahrenheit (49 degrees Celsius) and might even achieve 150 degrees Fahrenheit (66 degrees Celsius) or longer. As temperatures fall slightly after a couple of days, switching to supply more exceptional warmth causes temperatures to grow again. After the source of foods that are favored is consumed, thermophilic microbial activity decreases, and also the heap temperature drops.

3. Stage 3: **Mesophilic** monsters reassert command as temperatures fall below 104 degrees Fahrenheit (40 degrees Celsius). Besides microorganisms that flourish in such temperatures, soil invertebrates that decompose plant material start repopulating the heap. This last decomposition stage can last months or weeks, based on the length of time you allow your mulch"heal" until you use it. Temperature from the heap typically matches with the ambient air temperatures.

Handling the heat

Knowing these temperature stages and handling a thermophilic compost heap gives you the capacity to generate usable mulch immediately. All substances finally break down in trendy, unmanaged mulch piles too; however, decomposition happens quicker with high temperatures. Furthermore, should you want to destroy weed seeds or plant pathogens throughout the entire process, developing a sexy, thermophilic heap is indispensable.

Following are some tips for coping with a sexy heap:

◊ Require its temperature: Utilize a compost thermometer to maintain your own pile's temperature every day. Record it into a laptop or spreadsheet, and over time you will find a sense of how long phases take together with your composting components and techniques.

◊ Size it directly: Compost piles need mass to self-insulate and keep high temperatures during thermophilic composting. The minimal size would be 3 x 3 x 5 ft (1 cubic yard or one cubic meter) around 5 x 5 5 x 5 ft (1.5 cubic meters). This dimension enables the substance to self-insulate and isn't hard to turn to get an average gardener. Bigger sizes impair airflow into the middle of the heap.

◊ Twist, blend water: Temperatures fall as supplies of air, food, and water are drained. Twist the pile to aerate, mixing undecomposed components onto the exterior to the middle, or adding moisture can promote temperatures to grow and encourage faster decomposition. Sooner or later, food supplies are tired, and turning the heap no more promotes temperatures.

◊ Destroy pathogens and weed seeds: Many plant pathogens are ruined if temperatures stay between 130 and 140 degrees Fahrenheit (54 to 60 degrees Celsius) for 72 hours. Most weed seeds have been destroyed when subjected to temperatures over 131 degrees Fahrenheit (55 degrees Celsius) for 72 hours.

◊ Do not overheat: Heat your heap above 170 degrees Fahrenheit (77 degrees Celsius) for over a couple of hours isn't recommended since it inhibits many microbial actions and melts down the decomposition procedure.

If the heap is too warm, make it into aerating the heart and release warmth build-up.

4 COMPOSTING ABOVEGROUND OR UNDERGROUND

I wear a T-shirt that proclaims: Compost Happens. Since compost does look to"just happen," it is also a natural skill to understand, since this chapter explains. Heap up substance at a freestanding heap or bury your kitchen bits. Voilá! You are officially a composter. This chapter also clarifies the differences between aerobic (with air) and anaerobic (without oxygen) decomposition and supplies necessary actions to execute both kinds.

Composting With no Container

Composting with no boundaries of a container occurs in two standard manners: caked in a freestanding heap or below ground into a pit.

Freestanding piles are only that: heaps of natural thing piled up with no enclosure to corral them. Underground composting, better-called pit or trench composting, entails digging a pit, throwing on your material, and covering it up with dirt.

The following are the benefits and pitfalls connected with no-bin composting. No-bin composting is especially advantageous under these conditions:

◊ Should you like to test your hands in the home with as little investment as possible, it will not get much more economical than a heap of leaves and grass clippings or even a pit in the floor filled with kitchen pieces! It's possible to acquire experience with these approaches, then decide whether you need to"update" into a container.

◊ If you've plenty of lawn area and elbowroom, freestanding heaps are all beautiful. (It helps if you do not have looky-loo neighbors to peer with dismay on your mounds of organic issue.)

◊ For those who have lots and lots and lots and plenty of organic matter, bigger freestanding piles called windrows can suit you. Consult with the sidebar"Dealing together with windrows" for more about this.

◊ If the floor is simple to dig the trench, home is a viable option.

◊ n case you wish to get rid of kitchen scraps without bringing insects, trench composting will the tip (see the subsequent section, "Maintaining Your Binless Compost Critter-Free" for further information).

◊ In case you would like to mulch at the website of prospective planting regions, either way, it is excellent, and you do not need to transfer containers from year to year.

No-bin composting has its drawbacks, too. They comprise the following:

◊ Sprawling heaps of organic matter might seem cluttered unless, of course, you want to watch big heaps of leaves, grass, and plant trimmings psychologist into smaller piles of chocolate-brown compost. (Beauty is in the eye of the beholder.)

◊ Though you might do your very best to keep a clean place, there is no reliable method to keep insects from freestanding piles. Rodents, raccoons, dogs, foxes, badgers, and many others can gladly root about looking for something yummy to eat. (See the subsequent section"Maintaining Your Binless Compost Critter-Free" for more about this.)

◊ If your floor is tough, rugged, and hard to dig, then you would have to be made to select trench composting on a routine basis. Crazy!

A problem of AirConditioning versus Anaerobic Composting

Two broad types of germs absorb and decompose organic matter: aerobic (those who want atmosphere) and anaerobic (people who don't). This section enables you to know how these germs function and guides you in deciding which kind of home is ideal for your personality.

Aerobic composting: Maintaining everything

Most people who snore do this aboveground. It is the easiest method to begin with since all that is needed is a heap of an organic thing. Aerobic composting is the principle at work in aboveground composting surroundings -- if it happens in a freestanding heap or inside a container that offers airflow, like a bin having either side or even a tumbler with aeration holes.

Aerobic HOT compost	Anaerobic COOL compost
e.g. 3-Bay System	e.g. black council bin
Fueled by OXYGEN & moisture.	Fueled by BACTERIA & moisture
Turned weekly	Not turned
Large (at least 1 cubic metre)	Small (less than 1 cubic metre)
Quick Ready in 6 weeks	Slow Ready after 6 months
Kills pathogens & weeds	Can spread pathogens & weeds

Air is the most indispensable component in cardiovascular disease. If you have ever jumped and thumped via an aerobic workout course and discovered yourself looking out for air, then you understand firsthand that oxygen must exercise at maximum ability. The identical principle applies to nitric oxide on your mulch heap -- oxygen is vital to optimum functioning.

Ensuring aerobic organisms get sufficient air

Provided that lots of atmospheres can be obtained, aerobic decomposers work quicker and better than their anaerobic counterparts, supplying you with finished compost onto a quicker timetable. However, because creatures deplete the supply of oxygen in the present pores and spaces between pieces of organic matter, the decomposition procedure slows.

To maintain your decomposers functioning at a maximum rate, you might choose to integrate some kind of aeration help during your first heap construction. One means to do so is to heap organic substances in addition to a recycled delivery pallet

Continue to keep an eye on your heap's advancement and make alterations as required. If you become aware of the elevation of your mulch pile shrinking (it might shrink up to a foot inside a couple of days of its first structure), you can restate your aerobicizers by providing your heap a new extract of oxygen. You can accomplish that in a few ways:

◊   Switch your heap completely. Fork a freestanding stack into an adjoining place or flip the contents of a bin to another. When with a tumbler, twist it.
◊   Stir organic things frequently. Use a pitchfork or an aerating instrument to stir up things. You might want to do that every day for optimum results.

It is not strange to locate pockets of anaerobic composting happening in an abysmal heap that is intended to be aerobic-only. If mulch is still emitting a terrible odor, such as rotten eggs or ammonia, then it is too moist or too"green" using a thick, damp layer of grass clippings, fresh plants, or alternative nitrogen-rich organic thing that was not thoroughly blended with warm, carbon-rich substances, like straw or leaves. These solid masses do not allow air to flow, and nitric oxide is all prepared and ready to carry over.

Along with being unpleasant to operate around, poisonous compost scents can annoy neighbors, thus head off possible problems by mixing your initial batch of compost with proper quantities of nitrogen and carbon ingredients.

Aerobicizers : to bring to good physical condition through aerobics

Reaping the benefits of heat and character's cologne

Aboveground aerobic decomposers can resist higher temperatures compared to their cerebral counterparts, and they create heat for a by-product of the action. Not all of the aboveground piles are"warm," but if circumstances are into the decomposers' liking, temperatures on your heap heating up sufficiently to destroy weed seeds and seeds.

Probably the most potent feature of aerobic composting is the fact that it is a sweet-smelling job. A well-constructed compost heap does not smell bad. In reality, it creates a refreshing earthy odor, such as kicking leaves up during a stroll through the forests. Specialized aerobic bacteria called actinomycetes exude that pleasant odor for a byproduct of the decomposing activities.

Anaerobic decomposition: functioning with no atmosphere

Underground Allergic organisms operate with oxygen; therefore, many cerebral composting (at the least the sort that is done on purpose) occurs underground in pits or trenches. (That is why common names for southern composting include trench composting or pit composting.) Mostly, you dig a hole, fill it with the organic thing, and seal it with a layer of dirt. Anaerobic decomposers get to operate, without the demand for new O2 infusions out of you.

When anaerobic is advantageous

Anaerobic organisms operate at slower speeds than their aerobic moves, and it is not possible to track their improvement without digging to the pit and poking about. Sadly, this is sometimes an odious experience! Anaerobic organisms, unlike the sweet-smelling actinomycetes I explain previously, exude noxious gas for a by-product of the exertions. And since they operate in colder weather states, marijuana seeds and plant compounds are not destroyed.

Despite all these pitfalls, in certain instances, anaerobic composting is the ideal thing to do. It may satisfy you if some of the following apply:

◊   You are looking to eliminate a one time load of moist, possibly rancid, or pest-attracting toilet waste, like you, would collect after an afternoon spent canning fruits or veggies, cleansing freshly caught fish, or even coordinating a sizeable social gathering which creates food bits.

◊   Dig a pit ahead of this event, and you will be ready to eliminate waste. Paper napkins and dishes may go in using all the food scraps!

◊   Pulling spent garden crops in the conclusion of autumn leaves one with a massive heap of organic matter that you do not have the time or space to handle during winter.

◊   Aboveground composting of kitchen scraps with no sealed container is not permitted where you reside.
◊   You are not keen on the look of a mulch place on your landscape; however, you prefer not to ship your organic waste into a landfill.
◊   You need to enhance soil fertility and structure at a near garden bed.
◊   ou do not have the time to track the moisture or air requirements -- let alone flip -- an aboveground mulch pile.

Considering the hardness of the floor into consideration

I believe that getting an anaerobic composting convert is dependent upon where you reside and how simple it's to dig holes in the floor. I am a desert gardener in which the floor is tough, rugged, compacted, and may even supply an impervious hardpan layer simply to demonstrate the gardener who is boss. I dig a planting hole above a span of times, since I soak the ground with dirt and dirt out a couple of inches of dirt at one time, using a well-worn pickax. Voluntarily digging more pockets simply to throw into rotting organic matter isn't something that I will muster any excitement for!

On the flip side, I have got an arid-land gardener buddy who clinics anaerobic composting inside her garden beds, and in which the enhanced dirt is loose and easy to use. She digs a pit, tucks inside her entire day's worth of kitchen scraps, and covers it up. She does not wish to retrieve usable compost but lets the organic thing to rust set up to boost her backyard beds as time passes.

Making a Pile Aboveground

Developing a freestanding heap is the simplest way to split into composting. This segment covers the basics to give you a good notion of this procedure.

Where to blog the heap

Location is all about based on realtors, and therefore it's with your mulch pile. A perfect place is unethical (so substances do not dry), does not get overrun with rain (so substances do not become soggy), also within reach of the hose. It should provide adequate space for one to operate comfortably. Compost at least several feet from the buildings; thus, moisture in a heap does not seep to foundations. Aboveground composting in a couple of straightforward steps Construct a freestanding heap at least 3 feet x 3 feet x 5 feet (1 cubic yard or one cubic meter) around five cubic feet (1.5 cubic meters). This size provides sufficient mass for its organic thing to self-insulate and preserves warmth and moisture for those microorganisms swallowing it.

Chop, shred or split as a lot of your natural matter as you can into little pieces. The bigger the pieces, the quicker the speed of decomposition.

Follow these simple Actions to create your heap:

1. Distribute 4 inches (10 centimeters) of woody, luminous, or rough brown components, like corn, corn stalks, or dead perennial stalks, as the heap's base. This tough coating promotes aeration.
2. Sprinkle each layer with warm water as you build the heap, so it has the dampness of a wrung-out sponge. Also, sprinkle in a couple of handfuls (or even shovelfuls) of indigenous dirt here and there (you do not need to include dirt with each coating).
3. Distribute 4 to 5 inches (10 to 13 centimeters) of brownish substances, including dry leaves or shredded paper.
4. Spread 2-3 inches (5 to 8 centimeters) of green stuff, for example, spent garden crops and grass clippings.
5. Continue alternating layers of greens and reds, moistening as you possibly construct. End with a layer of browns at the top. You've got the option of covering the pile with a tarp. It will help maintain materials from drying in humid regions.

In moist climates, it averts the heap from becoming too moist and turning anaerobic.

Whenever your compost will be prepared to use

The duration of time required to acquire finished compost fluctuates dependent on the way you mix up the first components (forms of components, size of particles(and humidity levels) and just how much rotation and remoistening you opt to do following the heap is constructed.

In case you are in no rush for compost, then you can leave the heap sit is. But to jumpstart the decomposition procedure, include a fresh burst of oxygen needed (see the prior section"Ensure aerobic organisms get sufficient atmosphere" for specifics). Twist the compost to combine materials on the exterior of the heap into the inside so that which decomposes at a comparable speed.

Should you do nothing farther after constructing your heap, in three to six weeks, you are going to have the ability to harvest a few finished composts from the ground and center. Further decomposition (without rotation or moistening) may take a year or even longer. Typical decomposition period to acquire ample finished mulch out of a"well-constructed" heap that's frequently reversed and remoistened is roughly two to three weeks.

Digging a Hole (Pit or even Trench Composting)

If you reside where grinding holes in the earth aren't any big deal (lucky you), the following advice makes it possible to put in anaerobic composting for your repertoire.

Where to site the hole

Since appearance is not a problem as it may be using aboveground composting, it is possible to trench compost nearly anywhere that's handy and simple that you dig. Make sure that you understand where underground utility lines operate before digging. Excellent options to consider include regions where you would like to put in an upcoming blossom, vegetable, or herb garden, or even between rows of modern garden beds. Steer clear of wet locations or low areas with moist soil or lousy drainage.

Stay away from existing root programs when digging composting holes. Tree and tree roots readily extend to double the diameter of the aboveground canopy! Slicing through origins using a spoonful creates simple wounds for diseases and pests to get into, finally weakening and potentially killing your plant life. If you are unsure just how far roots might have spread, adhere to grinding compost trenches in garden beds.

Pit composting in a couple of straightforward measures

Determined by what you would like to attain, you can use many distinct procedures of pit or trench composting, including digging random holes, filling trench rows in garden beds, or even rotating trenches within a three-year interval to enhance an enlarged planting region. Utilize the original southern trench compost recipe, which follows for whatever way you select.

Filler up

Deep and wide to dig is dependent upon how much organic thing you must compost, what type of substance it's (landscape waste vs. kitchen waste), how simple it's to dig and if digging pests may be a problem (see the section"Maintaining Your Binless Compost Critter-Free" for more about the latter).

If you would like to recover finished mulch from the pit eventually, then understand that the more profound it's, the harder it's to eliminate. Scooping out completed compost out of lengthy, shallow trenches that are around 1 to 2 feet (30 to 60 centimeters) deep is much simpler than retrieving it in deeper holes with extreme sides.

1.	Dig the pit or trench, piling the dirt which you eliminate.

2.	Adhere to the sooner instructions for cardiovascular disease. Beginning with browns at the floor, alternate layers of green and brown stuff, moistening as you construct. Distribute a 1-inch (2.5-centimeter) coating of your booked dirt between layers of greens and reds.

3.	Cover 4 to 6 inches (10 to 20 centimeters) of dirt. If you plan to recover the mulch afterward, mark the region with a rock or other reminder.

Putting trenches between garden rows

If you grow flowers, flowers, or vegetables in straight rows with loads of distance between them and fulfill composting trenches between those pops. Since the organic matter from the trenches decomposes, nutrition becomes available for plants that are nearby. Dig trenches early in the planting year before vigorous roots extend in the region. Alternately, dig trenches in the conclusion of the growing season, therefore substance is decomposed by another planting season.

Organizing trenches for famished plants

Particular plants thrive on land that is full of organic matter and also water-holding substance, especially sweet beans, runner beans, zucchini (courgettes from the United Kingdom), pumpkins, and squash.

Six to eight weeks before planting, dig a trench or pit in which you intend to develop these plants, 18 inches (45 centimeters) deep. Fill with toilet waste, paper, manure, as well as other retentive stuff, then top with a 6-inch (15-centimeter) coating of dirt, heaping it up to create a mound. From the time your planting season rolls around, the website may have settled and get prepared for seeds or transplants.

Rotating trenches with planting regions

This procedure makes it possible to build decent garden soil as time passes by rotating trench composting regions with planting regions and pathways that permit entry to your plants.

Split the gardening area into three equal regions: 1 for developing crops, you for pathways to get the crops, and you for trench composting. In the conclusion of the three decades, you will have improved dirt in the whole location and get prepared to repeat the procedure. Organic matter from the dirt disappears through the activity of decomposer organisms; therefore, it requires constant replenishment.

This approach also helps with an old gardening practice known as crop rotation, where annual blossoms and fruits are intentionally grown in various locales from the backyard -- or calibrated -- every season to stop the build-up of soil-borne insects and diseases.

Whenever your compost will be prepared to use

The rate of decomposition underground is dependent on factors like those related to jelqing decomposition, like the ingredient combination, size of pollutants, and moisture level. The procedure could take anywhere from a few months to a year or even more.

Maintaining Your Binless Compost Critter-Free

This header is somewhat misleading. If you are composting aboveground at a freestanding heap, I am unaware of some surefire procedures to keep fleas at bay should they choose to see (assuming you are not likely to encircle your mulch area with electrical fencing and stand guard 24/7). The best deterrent is to continue kitchen scraps from freestanding piles. Even with scraps, a few higher-ups about the food chain could be attracted to succulent grubs or other insects that inhabit the subsequent phases of your rotting organic matter.

If you would like to compost kitchen scraps without even creating or purchasing an enclosed bin, alerting them into decompose anaerobically is the option. Discourage digging pests out of uprooting your yummy bits by merely covering the organic thing with a high layer of soil at least 2 inches (15 centimeters) thick (8 inches [20 centimeters] is preferable), adjusting the thickness of your pit to adapt the surface. Alternately, pay for the natural thing by something substantial that insects can not drift apart, like a boulder, coating of bricks, or sending pallets. Spreading a part of hardware cloth, chain link fencing, or poultry cable across the pit is just another option -- animals do not like to acquire their claws and feet stuck in the cable.

5 WORKING WITH COMPOST CONTAINERS

A great thing concerning the composting procedure is there are many distinct strategies to perform it. As I describe in previusly, then you can elect for a free-estanding mulch pile or just buried underground. Or you may elect for a bark container to get longer... well, included... approach.

This chapter covers all you want to learn about composting containers, beginning with helping you determine if containers are ideal for your situation, then covering the advantages and disadvantages of tumblers and bins. I provide you with ideas for picking one of the kitchen composters (made to take care of regular food scraps) and also talk about how to take care of wildlife that visits home improvement operations. The chapter finishes with features to mull over if purchasing a made compost container.

Composting at a Container (Or Three or Two)

Mother Nature does not sew her natural debris from containers; nevertheless, fragrant black humus -- the most favorable consequence of her effective composting procedure -- ensures forest floors. Why should you purchase or construct a container to corral your home attempts? Honestly, you do not need to. Freestanding piles work the work just fine, without a specific difference exists between natural thing rotting at a heap along with natural thing rotting in a container. However, since you find within this segment, you will find reasons why limiting organic matter into its quarters could be advantageous to you.

When using containers would be greatest

Acceptable landscape aesthetics differ extensively by individual, community, and community norms. If you are lucky to live where local authorities promote home composting to decrease solid waste delivered to landfills, you might be surrounded by inviting neighbors that also compost. (I love to picture the day when composting replaces automobiles as the newest"keeping up with the Jones's" behavior: "Honey neighbors included that a third bin. Get out there and build us different!")

On the flip side, you might be surrounded by people who are less enthused and do not wish to see that your mounds of organic matter by their chimney or backyard. Using containers which conceal organic thing with fully enclosed containers or sides which you could tuck into out-of-view places forestalls possible complaints.

Other Fantastic reasons to use containers on your efforts comprise the following:

◊ Containers maintain your stockpiles of dried substances, like leaves, straw, and sawdust, under command till you want them. Without some kind of holding unit, the carefully gathered ingredients may wind up scattered across the lawn next time a mighty wind blows.

◊ Maintaining kitchen scraps pests and in out is yet another significant benefit provided by containers that are entirely enclosed and comprise secure lids. Read"Keeping Wildlife Out Your Container" later in the chapter for additional information.

◊ In regards to active composting, keeping the overall size and contour of your first pile of components is simpler within the boundaries of containers. When compost substances have enough mass (at least one cubic yard [1 cubic meter]), they are better able to self-insulate to keep consistent humidity levels and high temperatures state that rate decomposition.

◊ Entirely enclosed bins assist organic things to keep moisture, a feature that is useful if you reside in an arctic climate. Decomposition slows down whenever the mulch heap dries out.

◊ In case you reside in a rainy climate, then enclosed bins maintain significant rains from soaking natural things. Wet stacks turn plump and polyunsaturated.

◊ Some bins provide insulating properties that help boost and maintain high temperatures indoors.

Sorting your composting design

Because I cite at the onset of the chapter, you don't require a container to create compost, and you are still studying, I presume that you have determined a container is logical for you. The queries in this section enable you to get started sorting out your options to discover the very best container for your individual needs.

How much money would you wish to invest in?

Lots of styles of containers that are manufactured are showing in the market as the notions of green living, sustainability, and composting profit in popularity. Consider the benefits and pitfalls of the containers that are manufactured I comprise later in this phase to choose whether their cost is acceptable for your financial plan.

You do not need to buy a costly container to begin. There are lots of container choices you can produce quite readily (even when you're not handy with resources) utilizing recycled materials, like 55-gallon, vinyl, food-grade drums using tight-fitting lids. Drill drainage holes at the base or cut off the bottom entirely, which also makes it effortless to pick the drum up and then place it apart when it is time to harvest or turn the compost.

How much organic matter are you going to process?

You might have moved into a new house and wish to begin a backyard, but you don't have any clue just how much organic matter your landscape and family will create. Or you might have resisted copious amounts of grass clippings throughout the summer and subsequently switched into the hills of leaves in fall (and compensated to get your garbage disposal firm to haul away it, based on where you reside), and you've got a fantastic estimate of the sum of organic matter your family produces.

No matter your scenario, it might allow you to consider composting in containers because of a"modular" system. If you are unsure how much organic thing you will possess, start with one square bin in the options I explain in Chapter 6, like concrete blocks, transport pallets, or perhaps straw bales. As you get experience and become bitten from the mulch"bug," you can quickly extend your performance. The square shape makes it a cinch to put in a second or third adjacent bin. The three-bin composting way is excellent for calculating a great deal of organic matter (see the section"Bins of all kinds" later in this chapter).

How much distance have you got to get a composting region?

Have a look at potential places on your landscape, and then gauge whether containers will match in the regions you are considering. Variable in elbow space for comfortable motion, such as turning the heap by hands or filling a wheelbarrow or cart using finished compost.

Many regional authorities or homeowner associations might have limitations on composting actions, like"no kitchen scraps " or"bins can not be observed from the road." Even though a three-bin system created from transport pallets can stand out, you will find different options you can tuck in an out-of-sight corner.

Besides, I offer you many different approaches for disposing of kitchen bits from the area"Toilet composters" later in this chapter.

Checking Your Options

This section describes features of distinct container designs, such as tumblers, bins, and kitchen composters. There are many options to suit unique scenarios. If something doesn't grab your attention, get active on the drawing board devising a brand new fashion!

Taking a twist with tumblers

Soil organisms decomposing your natural thing need a continuous source of oxygen to work at maximum possible, as describes. Additionally, mixing organic substances on the exterior of a heap into the interior that everything decomposes equally is a fantastic practice. Tumbling composters are intended to do precisely that: You either rotate or fall them to ease the use of oxygen and also the mixing of components without even swinging a pitchfork or bending the heap using an abysmal tool.

A fundamental tumbler design is shaped just like a canister, which you roll around the lawn. Other designs incorporate a large drum that rests on its left-handed rack using a hand crank to flip this and more compact components that you grip and twist since they break on somewhat concave pads onto the floor.

One issue I have experienced using tumblers is that new, moist stuff sometimes clumps to a compacted substantial chunk over the first day or two of rotating. The massive blob of organic things sheds out on the advantages of aeration provided by tumbling. Since the substances tumble inside, they drop and break from the pole, which will help to stop clods by forming. When you've got a different tumbler design, you might split any clods which sort using an instrument or your gloved hands. An oft-touted benefit of tumblers is they make it simple to turn mulch.

In theory, that is correct; however, in training, an oversized tumbler filled with damp organic matter isn't lightweight and needs the power to rotate. A correctly moistened composting effort begins out using 40 to 60% water. How readily you may turn the device is dependent on its weight and style, just how much and which kind of organic matter it is full of (fresh, moist compost weighs over a dry straw, for example), and also some other physical limitations you might have. If you want the idea of a tumbler but haven any constitutional concerns, locate fellow composters in the town that will allow you to choose their tumblers outside for a spin. Request garden clubs. Many gardens available to people also open their composting places.

Do not be bashful. I have never met with a composter who did not delight in sharing stories in their composting encounters.

You could also think of a bigger tumbling unit that is simpler to rotate. But composting is the most effective (providing you finished compost faster) as soon as the majority of organic thing starts outside at least one cubic yard (1 cubic meter) in size (3 ft tall by 3 feet wide by 3 ft deep, or one meter every single way). If a container is much smaller, then the procedure will take more. It can be true of almost any container fashion, not merely tumblers. The significance of container dimensions is discussed in the faucet"Examining a tumbler."

Eventually, a tumbler's enclosed sides foil bugs from rooting throughout the natural thing for kitchen scraps. In case the tumbler stays on the floor, make sure that its accessibility panels fasten firmly. (Some creatures are powerful smart at opening items.) Tumblers that remaining stands are much more pest-proof, but besides, they need entrance doors.

Bins of all kinds

I specify"bin" quite widely with this particular discussion. Nearly any container which is not a tumbler falls to the bin group. The following are attributes to take into account.

Closed or open

Open bins are only that: Some blend of the best, sides, and bottom are all open into the atmosphere, precipitation, as well as insects. Examples include home-made square bins made from shipping pallets and fabricated round enclosures made from lightweight recycled vinyl with pre-formed venting holes, like the Presto GEOBIN (test it out in www.prestoproducts.com/consumer/garden/bins.htm). Open bins have several benefits:

◊ They are more straightforward and less costly to vertical, with fewer building materials demanded.
◊ Adding more compostables over the years is straightforward.
◊ Stirring up the combination with an aerating instrument is simple.
◊ The open floor underneath the bin enables soil organisms to obtain rapid entry, speeding decomposition.
◊ Open sides or an open surface benefit from complimentary water and air (and snow).
◊ However, they also have a few drawbacks:
◊ Open sides or an open surface allow stuff to dry out quickly or become overly moist, depending upon the climate.
◊ Pests have simple accessibility.
◊ The look of organic matter could be gruesome.

Like open containers, closed ones have a few advantages (Closed bins):
◊ Hide organic thing to get a tidier appearance
◊ Retain moisture and heat more evenly
◊ Inhibit pest manage (see"Keeping Wildlife Out Your Container" later in the chapter)

Following are some drawbacks to shut bins:
◊ They demand more stuff, which makes them more costly.
◊ Adding and obtaining organic substances is harder.
◊ They are usually smaller in dimension, therefore holding less natural substance.

Stationary versus aerodynamic

Stationery bins sit in 1 area for your length, if you don't employ time and attempt to reevaluate them. Cases contain a bin made from concrete blocks or even a wooden three-bin unit. Movable composters are free to"get up and go around the cottage." Or, even more correctly, you are free to move them all over your lawn with very little work. It is a great feature when you have only one container and wish to turn your compost regularly to aerate or remoisten it. Lift the container away from the heap, place it apart, and then fork or shovel the natural thing back in.

Multi-bin systems

Only 1 square bin may hold and create a substantial number of organic matter, and advantage of a standard square shape is that you may quickly add third or second adjacent bins to match changing demands for more extended space. (Or you'll be able to get rid of a bin for those who want less space) If you answer"yes" to some or All these questions, You Might feel comfortable beginning with just 1 square bin:
◊ Are you brand new to composting?
◊ Are you uncertain just how much organic substance your lawn and family will create?
◊ Are you uncertain just how much time and effort you need to enter composting?

When you get experience, it is possible to add adjoining third and second bins readily. You will eventually get to the composting outcome signal of a pal of mine that used six bins at a row in a neighborhood garden! From the time organic thing reached the previous bin, it had been dark, rich mulch prepared to integrate into the backyard.

Following are a few more questions to think about:

◊ Can you intend to keep compost piles during the year, including new substances, as they become accessible?

◊ Can your lawn and family generate a substantial amount of organic matter you wish to recycle?

◊ Would you like to create lots of fertilizer?

◊ Can you like turning organic substances available?

If you answered"yes" for some or all those questions, then you are a prime candidate to get a three-bin mulch system. Three squarish bins discuss conventional sidewalls. This design uses space economically, making it easy to switch organic material from 1 bin in the next. Mostly, you fill Bin #1 using organic thing and start it outside. When it is partially decomposed and prepared to twist, you change it in Bin #2 and then begin a fresh pile of new organic things in Bin #1. Once Bin #2 ton farther, you flip it in Bin #3 to complete off. And thus, the cycle persists.

Kitchen composters

Not many goods marketed as toilet composters create usable compost out of the kitchen waste. Some are just attractive holding components that combine unobtrusively with your kitchen décor till you have sufficient time to ditch the organic matter to your outside bin. Others, like bokashi composters, begin the decomposition ball rolling, but you have to finally move the organic thing outside, either into a compost pile or into a pit in the floor where it proceeds to invisibly to materials that enhance soil and supply nourishment to crops.

An exterior option for composting kitchen waste would be an undercover"-meals digester," like the Green Cone made to discourage pests. However, what can you do with kitchen scraps should you reside in an apartment or condominium without access to an outside area for composting? Look at harboring a bin of germs to chow down on your food waste. Called vermicomposting, this way is intriguing and potent. Worms eat at least half of their weight in food every day.

Consequently, in case you've got a pound of worms, then they will procedure approximately a half-pound of bits. If worms are not something, yet another indoor option that generates finished mulch is an electric-powered component that mixes and aerates almost all kitchen scraps, such as fish, poultry, and milk. Finished compost falls right to a holding tray in which it proceeds to heal, and you're able to get it when suitable.

I clarify these options (except that the bugs) for composting kitchen waste at much more detail in the subsequent sections.

Countertop crocks

You also might find it handy to design kitchen scraps destined to get your outside bin in a little countertop container in easy reach of food preparation areas. Resembling miniature trash cans or ice cubes, those components hold roughly a gallon's worth of bits (that is about 3.8 liters).

Search for crocks that contain pre-assembled claws and activated charcoal filters inside the lid to keep odors in check. Bad scents or fly invasions should not happen if you empty your container frequently -- every few days or weekly, based on what you are filling it together along with the temperature on your residence. Filters last around three weeks. Factor in the expense of replacement filters when making your purchase choice.

You do not need to get unique merchandise to repaint kitchen bits. Toss them in a plastic storage container with a tight lid and then keep it into the freezer to forestall any smells and flies. Transfer it to an outside compost performance when suitable. Rinse the container outside and put the water onto the compost heap contents.

Drizzle lemon juice, vinegar, or baking soda inside kitchen garbage collection containers to eliminate odors naturally.

Bokashi composting

Bokashi is a Japanese word referring to a procedure for fermenting organic things. Bokashi kitchen composting combines scraps using an inoculant (known as bokashi) of beneficial bacteria that accelerate regeneration anaerobically (without oxygen), while preventing the offensive smells standard of anaerobic decomposition. Bokashi inoculant is generally sold as sterile rice or corn bran embedded with germs and their food supply, like molasses. Bokashi containers do not create fertilizer. The closed method ferments (pickles) kitchen bits, beginning the breakdown of organic matter. In the conclusion of this fermenting interval, food scraps continue to be recognizable since they are pickled, not decomposed.

The last decomposition occurs outside after you bury the stuff from the dirt or even a compost bin. Consider these benefits and disadvantages to choosing if it's the bokashi process is ideal for you.

Below are the experts of using a bokashi program:

◊   The first indoor fermentation interval creates food waste of a lure for insects after moving it outside.
◊   Soil germs immediately break down, staying organic things after the substance is placed outside.
◊   Food wastes which need to be kept from conventional, open-to-the air (aerobic) compost bins, like milk and meat, can be placed at a bokashi container.
◊   The container controls only a tiny level of space.
◊   Liquid emptied off throughout the fermentation phase may be diluted and used as plant food.

Naturally, the bokashi program has its drawbacks, too. These contain the following:
◊   Purchasing bokashi is a continuing expense.
◊   Scraps need to be chopped into little pieces.
◊   Rotten or muddy scraps shouldn't be composted.
◊   Material needs to be buried outside at least eight to 12 inches deep in the soil or mulch heap after the first fermentation.
◊   Two or more containers will be required to keep processing pieces while the container ferments.

Bokashi composting demands an airtight container, using an optional spout in the foundation for draining liquid generated through fermentation. (Eliminate liquid or dilute 1 part liquid using 100 parts water and use it to fertilize plants) You can purchase containers or create your own out of a five-gallon bucket with a tight lid.
Input"bokashi composting" to your favorite online search engine to learn more about the procedure, such as locating bokashi inoculant and directions for generating and utilizing a bokashi container.

Green Cone

The Green Cone composter is occasionally called an inground food digester. It can take care of all kinds of kitchen waste and food scraps, such as legumes, fish, meats, milk farms, and oils. But if you are going to bring those things, fix the device from insects (see the trick later in this segment).

The Green Cone includes four components: a covered jar, two aboveground cones, along with a lid. Bury the ground, and each of those fantastic dirt organisms may scale right in and have to work breaking your scraps. Aboveground, the Green Cone resembles, well, a green cone. Within it's a second, smaller cone that fits firmly across the base portion to repel insects. You pop up your kitchen bits in the upper cone, with a lid.

The Green Cone was not supposed to make useable fertilizer. It is meant to recycle food scraps and also maintain them from the waste flow. Most substances will probably break down to carbon dioxide and fluids that disperse in the surrounding land. As an alternative, you may harvest residue which stays in the basket after 9 to 12 weeks and then insert it into your mulch pile or place it in your backyard.

The Principal Benefits of this Green Cone is it

◊   Keeps all of the kitchen scraps from this waste flow.
◊   It does not need mixing or turning.
◊   Requires restricted outdoor area to install.
◊
◊   The primary disadvantages of this Green Cone are it
◊   It does not create much usable compost.
◊   It requires excellent soil drainage and a sunny place to operate at peak efficiency.
◊   May bring digging pests.
◊   May fill with natural material quicker than decomposition happens. When the cone becomes 1/4 into 1/3 complete, organic thing (which can be wet and stinky) must be removed and buried in the backyard or other mulch pile. Running two components concurrently reduces this dilemma. An individual could be compelled to decompose while another is full of fresh planters.

To forestall insects digging into the Green Cone, wrap the basket from tight wire mesh, like hardware cloth, before hammering it. After installing the device, securely compact the surrounding land and protect it with rocks, bricks, or openings to dissuade creatures that are attracted to recently dug soil. If insects are an issue, restrict captivating components, such as beef, fish, and milk.

NatureMill

This automatic, electric-powered unit involves an upper room that retains food bits and a lower room for finished compost. A heater retains the top room's contents warm to ease decomposition. A fan pulls air in, and it leaves through an air filter to control aroma. The device's keyboard tells the engine when to run the top room's blending bar, which continues for a few moments at a time (that is the mesmerizing stage). When the organic thing has shrunk satisfactorily, the device sends it via a trap door into a holding tray at the bottom room. Additionally, it adheres to"treatment" farther until you are prepared to crop it. Meanwhile, you re the top room with more bits.

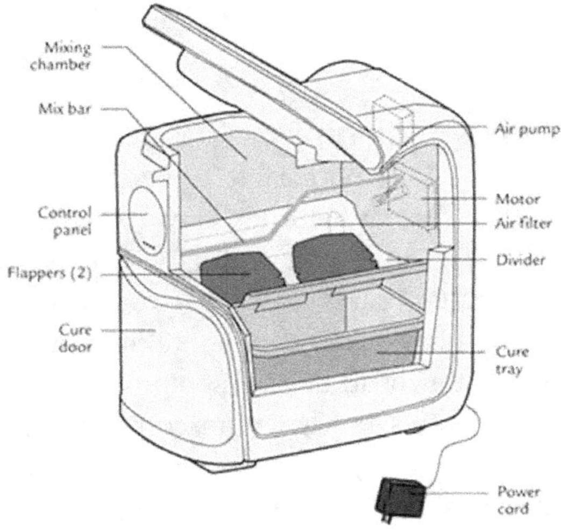

The many attractive features of this NatureMill composter is it
◊ Composts normal kitchen scraps along with beef, fish, milk, and oils
◊ Accommodates up to 4 lbs daily, to include scraps as often as you need
◊ Works quickly to turn bits into mulch
◊ Operates inside or outside (with electrical plug)
◊ Features a compact dimension -- 20 inches high x 20 inches x 12 inches broad (50.8 x 50.8 x 30.5 centimeters, respectively)

Following are a couple of disadvantages of this machine:
◊ The motor which turns the mixing pub is noisier compared to the device's continuing low hum.
◊ Scraps should be sliced into 4-inch bits.
◊ The device is significantly more expensive than any other option.

Keeping Wildlife Out Your Container

Depending on where your home is, creatures brought to your mulch pile might comprise cats, rodents, cats, foxes, raccoons, coyotes, badgers, and javelina. In certain areas, even bears might seem in backyards as development spreads in their collections, and standard food has become scarce.

Individuals are those typically benign on the creatures' land -- do not blame them for hunting food.

When crazy animals tangle with people, the creatures are typically the losers; therefore, it is much better to dissuade them in the get-go instead of attempt to modify their regular once they have discovered there is a common food source in your garden. You can accomplish it by eliminating particular ingredients in the compost and using bins

Eliminating enticing ingredients

Its odor, although not especially noticeable to people, may bring in undesirable critters into the heap, such as your pet. Cover kitchen pieces or vegetable garden trimmings are having an 8-inch coating of dry brown substances, like leaves, straw, or organic matter that is in the process of decomposing. Applying three or two side-by-side bins makes it simple. Pitchfork or shovel material stockpiled in 1 bin on the newly additional scraps in another bin. Employing bin features to exclude animals Producers of compost bins understand that creatures can be quite smart in regards to gaining access into the contents of the bin so that they design their bins with particular characteristics that keep critters out. The Subsequent bin fashions and attributes inhibit undesirable access:

◊ Entirely enclosed bins (including sturdy bottoms) with firmly manicured figurines
◊ Tumblers resting aboveground supports
◊ Little aeration holes covered with cable net
◊ Bin designs designed to discourage pests like the Green Cone (refer to the earlier segment)

If constructing your bins or changing less protected produced bins, these thoughts may help you prevent fleas from gaining entry:

◊ Cover aeration holes together with hardware cloth or wire mesh to prevent rodents from penetrating through. (Rodents chew plastic mesh)
◊ Construct timber bins with tight mesh wire sides and hinged wood, or fiberglass lids.
◊ Lay thick covers (like wood transport palettes) at the very top of big open bins to obstruct easy accessibility.
◊ Lay bricks along with easy-to-remove lids.

Bugs, rodents, and flies, oh my!

Insects are a necessary element of a wholesome compost pile, and thus don't sweat your existence.

Bugs

If did people become "bug-averse?" Creatures of all types that occupy the heap do not do much damage and can supply you with a significant sideshow. While I turn to mulch, lizards scurry closer across the cube wall to receive a peek at delicious offerings my pitchfork could have discovered. I do not even need to stand still; a daring lizard will rush, catch its meal, and go home with supper dangling out of the mouth. When I turn my back for a moment, birds hop about the heap, snapping up succulent white grubs found in finished mulch. Be looking to find out what interesting native monsters could be feasting on bugs out of the mulch pile.

Ants

Unlike slips, which set route for a moist heap, rodents like living quarters that are dry. Moistening and turning the heap often may send them packing. Some regular ants always appear to be scurrying via a mulch pile, and they are not a cause of concern. But in case you've got nasty biting snakes, then put them under control when possible so that they do not disperse colonies into other regions of your landscape. To get a standard pesticide Therapy, try one of these:

◊ Spinosad: This really can be a pesticide based on a naturally occurring soil bacterium. If you are an organic gardener, then start looking for an item which claims on its container which spinosad is the active ingredient also it's certified to be used in natural gardens.

◊ Orange peel slurry: To create a slurry, grind orange peels using plain water from a blender. Flood the ant mound together with the slurry instantly after making it so that it will not lose its potency.

◊ Boiling water: Pouring boiling water at the mound is just another option.

◊ Aromatic plant: The most pungent yet agreeable odor of a certain mint species (Mentha requiring) deters ants. You might discover it available as Corsican mint from the USA or pennyroyal mint from the U.K.

Flies

If you discover yourself with the issue of annoying pests, you are probably dealing with family flies. Flies are attracted to damp, rotting organic matter where they lay their eggs. Hatching fly larvae (known by the unpleasant-sounding moniker maggots) stay in a heap three to four times, guzzling down organic things before pupating and emerging as adult flies to repeat the cycle.

In case you've got annoying quantities of flies buzzing about, your heap needs focus. Evaluate Your heap's requirements and components to Ascertain whether You Have to employ these corrective steps:

◊ Twist the heap. This introduces oxygen dry out too wet heat or material up the heap. (Fly larvae expire in substantial temperatures) Make certain materials in the outer borders become worked to the center so that each has an opportunity to"feel the warmth."

◊ Insert more green nitrogen substances, like grass clippings or compost, to improve warmth amounts.

◊ Add more sterile carbon substances (such as leaves or straw) to counteract a wealth of too wet nitrogen compounds (like compost, grass clippings, along with coffee grounds).

◊ Regularly bury food bits inside the center of the heap or cover new developments using the 8-inch (20-centimeter) coating of leaves or straw.

Searching for a Composter: A Buyer's Guide

The most frequent shame I hear from anglers about composting in bins that are manufactured seems something like that: "It takes more than that I thought it might create finished compost." Regrettably, compost containers (although a number of the advertising materials that follow them) are not magic apparatus at which you fall in straw, wave your wand-like mulch thermometer, and presto -- outside clogs black stone! The fundamental demands of decomposer organisms should nevertheless be fulfilled, including a suitable mixture of nitrogen and carbon substances chopped into little bits, moisture and aeration throughout the procedure, and adequate mass to develop and maintain humidity levels. Your efforts in fulfilling these demands prefer the varieties of mesophilic and thermophilic organisms that do the majority of the job.

Whether tumblers or bins, containers possess shared characteristics, as explained in the next listing. Contemplating these options collections you on the Ideal path to Picking the container that is Ideal for the situation:

◊ Size: As comparison shopping, bear in mind that container dimensions are frequently the most limiting factor in its capability to create dirt quickly. In case the container retains greater than one cubic yard (1 cubic meter) of substances (the minimal dimensions for useful decomposition), you're still able to work with this. However, you have to handle the materials, moisture, air, and temperature regularly if you would like speedy compost, as you would using a freestanding heap or homemade bin. If you are in no rush and simply need a clean receptacle to include a rather modest number of natural leftovers, subsequently, container dimensions are much less significant a variable.

◊ Weight: When it is a tumbler, you need to have the ability to quickly rotate it if it is filled with the thick, wet organic thing. When it is not a tumbler, and you also use only one container, then it is lovely to have the ability to lift it up and away from the organic thing to place it apart for rotation or reloading.

◊ Height: Be sure that you can lift your pitchfork or shovel packed with organic substances to your container. It is generally less fatiguing to break your pitchfork or shovel around the face of the container because you drain that, instead of to hoist it up over shoulder level.

◊ Meeting required: Many bins need some assembly. Connectors like screws or screws usually consume more than vinyl tabs that crack or split after a year or two at extreme weather. Start looking for a sturdy, stiff structure. Loose connections may come aside and cause the container to fall when you are poking around in the middle of the bin using an instrument to aerate organic issues.

◊ Lids: Search for sufficiently high top openings to include new organic things. Can your loaded-up pitchfork or shovel fit with space to spare? Or do you want to use your hands-on material substances? Maybe you'd prefer a more compact entry door inside the lid, which you could turn open to throw from the afternoon's kitchen bits without removing the whole lid.

◊ Pest deterrents: Lids must tighten securely to safeguard against enterprising insects and powerful winds. At precisely the same time, you would like to have the ability to lift pliers to include more organic things without a great deal of fuss. Containers must be completely enclosed, such as a tight or solid wire-mesh underside. A few open-to-the ground containers possess optional bottoms that it is possible to purchase. Containers raised on racks above floor level will also be excellent pest deterrents; however, they still require safe lids to foil bottoms.

Check with your regional parks division, fish and game, wildlife, or any other all-natural resource management services for advice on local pest issues and advocated deterrents.

◊ Entry panels: Several units provide sliding trap doors in the base to provide entry to the finished mulch. Verify the measurements to find out if your spade will match indoors. Otherwise, you are going to want to scoop out mulch out or use a hand trowel. Some components have panels on several sides. In case the composter doesn't have any floor, lifting it and placing it aside for in the final product is usually simpler than poking about in tiny portholes.

◊ Aeration and drainage pockets: Air and water are all significant elements in composting. If containers are wholly enclosed, then there have to be some means for letting air in and moisture out. With drainage, then the contents of this container turn rancid and rancid, and the decomposition procedure slows.

6 SELECTING YOUR INGREDIENTS

I wear a T-shirt that proclaims: Compost Happens. Since compost does look All of the once-living things decompose finally, which means you could wonder if it matters what enters your mulch pile or just how much material you're using. If you are in no rush to acquire usable compost, then you do not need to be overly worried about those problems -- mulch occurs. But if you are a gardener who needs a great deal of crumbly compost earlier instead of later, knowing the fundamental hows and whys of choosing carbon-rich and nitrogen-rich natural things and combining them in the ideal percentage is valuable.

This chapter identifies the distinct organic substances accessible to place in your compost heap and enables you to find out the most effective proportions of every Additionally, and it covers all of the stuff which should certainly stick out from the heap! At length, tons of thoughts on locating free components (and keeping them) render you no explanations for exercising the nuclear issue!

Getting rid with Browns: Carbon-Rich Ingredients

Gardeners who Materials often reference carbon-rich substances as browns because nearly all of them are a variety of shades of brown. Sugar precious carbon substances offer energy for germs whenever they busily break your fundamental issue. Carbons for its compost heap (as a way of overall accessibility for the majority of people) contain tender leaves, woody plant trimmings, all kinds of paper goods, walnut, pine needles, and sawdust.

Dry leaves

Dry leaves are most likely the simplest brownish ingredient to utilize to get a start composter since they are already small parts of organic matter, which are simple to shred into tinier pieces should you select. They are also in plentiful supply in many areas and become quite adequate completed compost (known as leaf mold) all independently, with no inclusion of different substances. Just have a peek at some woodland floor to realize how it occurs. The local faucet" When life provides you leaves, create leaf mold" informs you how you can work with plenty of leaves to make moisture-enhancing compost.

Shredding leaves reduces their quantity, which makes it less challenging to stockpile considerable quantities to add to your mulch as required. Shred leaves by dispersing them throughout the grass and running them over using a lawnmower. No mower and lawn? Fill out plastic trash can half filled with leaves and then put a weed eater inside like a leaf shredder. (make sure you use protective eye equipment.)

Woody plant trimmings

Shrubs, trees, palms fronds, dead perennial stalks, Brussels sprout stalks, and dried cornstalks all fit into such a group. Split, chop and then scatter the substance as far as you can to accelerate decomposition. (Chapter 2 explains tools that assist for this.) But if you can not embarrass it little, do not worry; there is nothing wrong with yanking partly decomposed branches and twigs out of a completed compost pile to improve some other heap (maybe multiple times) till they are totally"gone" Another usage for woody substances: Distribute them in the base of a heap before building to market aeration.

Get some of your neighbors together and organize to handle your pruning tasks at precisely the same moment. Pile up all of your woody trimmings, then convene to get a notary celebration. Rent a chipper/shredder in the tool rental shop, and share the cost, labor, and outcomes.

Paper goods

Though I try to recycle up to my newspaper as you can, a lot remains abandoned for composting. Other paper products that are simple to shred or split comprise used paper towels, envelopes, paperboard (unwaxed food and cereal boxes), paper towel and toilet tissue rolls, plus paper.

Cardboard is slow to mulch, as well as also the denser stuff is difficult to tear, though it works nicely for soaking up extra moisture from wet ingredients. Stir it and combine it with fresh mulch or grass clippings, or put it on the base of a heap if you are composting at a moist region. Cardboard is simpler to address if you leave it lying about for a couple of days once the weather is moist; it rips easily, along with the dampness also lets you quickly get rid of any packaging tape instead of pulling those annoying pieces from your completed mulch later.

Straw

Made in the rest dried stalks of cereal grains (wheat, barley, rye, barley) following the grain was threshed and eliminated, straw can be used mostly for livestock bedding. It is used less often than hay because livestock feed since filler's nutrient value and digestibility is reduced. (See the section"Hay" later in this chapter to compare both.) You can use straw from the garden as compost; it is safer to work with than hay since it includes few marijuana seeds.

Pine needles

The most resinous coating on fibers may take some time to break, therefore use them at a limited amount. In case you've got a good deal of pine needles, then you can readily stockpile them gradually blend them with other organic substances. (Pine needles also make appealing and efficient mulch spread around garden beds)

Do not fret about pine needles' acidity unless you've got a good deal of these: Modest amounts have minimum impact on your compost heap or dirt.

Sawdust

Since sawdust has a substantial carbon to nitrogen (Vitamin C: N) ratio (more about which later in the phase), use it in the compost heap. Pairing an exclamation coating (no longer than an inch) between moist grass clippings, or blend handfuls completely with tons of different ingredients.

Atomic layers of sawdust squeeze to thick mats, so reducing the capability of water and oxygen to circulate throughout the heap. Additionally, decomposers begin to operate on sawdust because they do each other element, but due to the high carbon loading, they need copious quantities of nitrogen-rich substance over the time to process carbon. Sprinkling small sums of sawdust you create on your woodshop will not hurt the procedure; dumping substantial quantities in your local sawmill will close down it.

Try these alternate uses if you've got access to plenty of sawdust:
◊   Spread it on paths.
◊   Twist it to destroy weeds.
◊   Stockpile it alone at a holding place to simmer for a year or longer. Adding it into mulch piles because of carbon source afterward is safer.

Greening Up It: Nitrogen-Rich Ingredients

Nitrogen-rich substances are known as greens because nearly all of them are greenish. There are usually exceptions to any rule simply to keep you on your feet. Manure and coffee grounds are all nitrogen substances that happen to be brownish. Greens offer bodybuilding proteins to the germs crunching throughout your fundamental issue. Great green resources comprise kitchen scraps, grass clippings, leafy plant trimmings, and compost. Feathers, fur, and hair along with additional nitrogen sources to utilize.

Kitchen scraps

Aside from things listed in the area"Understanding which Materials to Prevent" later in this chapter, leftovers in the kitchen have been great additions to the mulch pile. You can do the environment a huge favor also, since kitchen waste not just pops up crap websites, but besides, it generates methane, a greenhouse gas, even because it decomposes. In the deal, you also conserve funds required to transfer and procedure that waste by incorporating the next scraps for your mulch:
◊   Coffee motives and utilized filters

◊   Condiments and sauces
◊   Corncobs
◊   Cut flowers
◊   Eggshells
◊   Fruit pits
◊   Fruit rinds and cores
◊   Nut cubes
◊   Shells from additives
◊   Stale or grated grain and bread products
◊   Tea and Tea totes
◊   Vegetables (cooked or raw)

Fruit pits, like eggshells, nutshells, and peppermint cubes, are slow to decompose. Crush or grind them before adding them to a compost pile, to accelerate the procedure.

Many regional municipalities might have limitations on incorporating food waste to start compost bins, even though enclosed or covered bins are often okay. Check for restrictions in your town.

Grass clippings

When I had to select a favorite composting ingredient, it'd probably be grass clippings. Pre-chopped into tiny bits from the mower and filled up with nitrogen and moisture, what's not to enjoy? Oh, I nearly forgot: Grass clippings turn slimy and smelly when left big piles or layered too densely, so combine them up with brownish materials whenever possible or distribute them out to dry for a couple of hours before blending them into your pile.

When organic gardening basics are all essential to you, along with the clippings that you utilize arise from neighbors or alternative resources, confirm the yards were not treated with chemical fertilizers or compost.

In case you don't want your grass clippings for composting, grasscycling is an effortless recycling substitute. All you need to do is allow the clippings to lie around the lawn after shaving!

Clippings decompose rapidly and reunite to 25% of the overall nutrition your lawn needs, which means that you can employ 25% less fertilizer to a lawn. A mower using a mulching feature will lower the size of grass clippings, and speeding decomposition.

Leafy plant trimmings, spent flowers, flowers, and veggies

As soon as your garden crops have finished generating for the season, then pull them out, block or split them into smaller bits, and throw them in the compost pile to recycle their content. The same holds for leafy trimmings from picture trees and shrubs. If plants present pest or disease issues, it is far better to make them outside of the mulch mix (see"Understanding which Materials to Prevent" later in this chapter).

When bracken ferns have dispersed invasively on your garden or landscape, then the greenery creates a superb addition to the compost pile once you cut it in the growing period. Do not include the origins, however, because this challenging plant could be an issue in gardens. But aim to complete picking bracken ferns to your heap by early summer, due to mid to late summer that the leaves have generated spores which could be harmful when inhaled.

Weeds -- leaves just!

A wholesome crop of germs, though annoying, is a good supply of iodine. Return those nutrients into your garden in the place where they belong by bettering your possessions. Make sure that you don't include things like seed heads or recurrent roots that could synthesize.

Livestock manure

Chicken, bunny, duck, geese, horse, goat, llama, rabbit, sheep, and poultry manures are secure to add to mulch. Manure contains very tiny quantities of macronutrients (nitrogen, phosphorus, and potassium) that plants need, in addition to essential micronutrients (trace elements), including boron, iron, calcium, and zinc. Though mulch adds only slightly to the general nutrient level of the mulch, it will provide solid organic matter and also lots of parasitic activity.

Based on the animals' daily diet, a few manures may include a good deal of marijuana seeds, so if you are getting a load of mulch right from the origin (so to speak), inquire regarding the creature's eating habits. (See the subsequent section, "Hay.") Horse manure, individually, may be filled with seeds that pass through the creature's digestive tract. If you don't mulch having a hot heap which reaches temperatures over 131 degrees Fahrenheit (55 degrees Celsius) for 72 hours, then seeds can last composting and sprout, getting a nuisance in the backyard. If you are using manure right in your backyard, it has to be at least six weeks to be secure. Fresh manure, with being rancid, comprises concentrated nitrogen, which can"burn" plant roots and tender tails or protect against seed germination. (Yellow dog stains in your yard are a visual illustration of the effectiveness of nitrogen-rich waste).

It's possible to add fresh mulch directly onto your compost pile since it is nitro-gen-rich, sexy, and moisture-laden. But, it may throw away the workings of a mulch pile when inserted in plentiful amounts. Should you happen to Acquire super-fresh moist planters, utilize it at the following manners:

◊ Let it dry out a bit before adding it into your mulch, then mix it with a broad selection of additional components.
◊ Compost it at a heap alone.
◊ Distribute fresh mulch across backyard beds in autumn, letting it rust du-ring the winter months.
◊ Spread it around beds which lie fallow (that's, that are not utilized for de-veloping whatever) six weeks to a year before planting.

Digging mulch to the upper layer of dirt promotes faster decomposition. Never distribute fresh mulch on a backyard that's already implanted, since its"warm-th" can destroy plants. Nor would you want it to dab fresh foliage. Just how long to wait until planting is dependent upon the freshness of this manure and just how fast it decomposes on your climate. Always wear protective equip-ment (gloves and gloves, in addition to a dust mask when the manure is dusty and dry) if collecting or dispersing manure. And regardless of how secure you are, excellent hygiene remains crucial: make sure to clean your hands thorou-ghly and carefully wash beneath your nails after managing manure.
Manure got in bulk by farms, stables, and animal owners (instead of the type you make it at a plastic bag in the garden center) may comprise more than me-rely nitrogen-rich substance. Mixed in can be carbon-rich bedding material, including straw or sawdust. That is perfectly fine -- it is a mulch pile in the procedure even before going back home with the merchandise!

Pet bedding
Little pets like hamsters, rabbits, guinea pigs, and gerbils are bedded down with paper, hay, or shavings. Also, this bedding is a beneficial addition to the mulch pile.

Feathers
After I was a tiny child playing with softball, a teammate's father spread a coa-ting of poultry feathers (his loved ones raised eggs available) within our infield in late autumn. Chicken feathers fluttered about in an enchanting snowfall un-til actual snow packaged down them to winter. I can not demonstrate it helped my team win some matches, but the subsequent spring, we all played with the lushest, greenest, most coveted bud of any group in the area.

In case you don't reside near or have use of some poultry farm, then you can empty any undesirable feather pillows, down comforter, or feather-filled cushions in your residence and blend in the feathers because you fill out your compost bin.

Fur and hair

Wash your hairbrush (also Fido's and Fluffy's) within the bin. If you are desperate for nitrogen, then ask your favorable barber, stylist, or pet groomer to help save a stash whenever they sweep up. Fur and hair Sometimes take some time to clot if piles are not kept to decompose knowingly.

Hay

Bales of hay have been constituted of seeds and legumes, including alfalfa, red clover, or timothy, which are increased as feed for livestock. Foliage is cut still green and left to dry at the area until machines squeeze it to rectangular bales. To preserve its nutrient significance for animals and also to reduce spoilage, hay should dry and fast, with limited exposure to sunlight and rain. Nitrogen content varies dependent upon the crops increased (legumes such as alfalfa and clover include more oxygen than grasses) along with the drying procedure. An issue to think about before adding hay into a compost pile is its marijuana content.

Based on exactly where and hay is grown and processed, then it might have a bumper crop of marijuana seeds that endure the mulch pile to sprout on your backyard. If you do not understand the origin along with the hay is not licensed as weed-free, search alternate forms of nitrogen to your mulch.

Understanding which Materials to Prevent

Composting is not a free-for-all. You can not throw in anything and all you run across waste-wise and anticipate it to create usable healthful compost. Some substances do not qualify as compost components since they include pathogens, bring insects, or lead to other issues. Save hassles and headaches by maintaining the following things from your home improvement:

◊ Meat, bones, grease, oils, fats, or milk goods: They turn rancid and pungent, and entice puppies, cats, raccoons, foxes, and rodents.

◊ Feces: Waste out of puppies, cats (such as polyunsaturated cat litter), pet animals, dinosaurs, and people could contain parasites that are transferrable to and infectious to people.

◊ Charcoal grill or dirt ash: All anglers must leave these alone since they feature sulfur oxides and other substances you do not need to move to your backyard.

◊ Wood ashes: Wood ashes are alkaline. If you garden in which lands are alkaline (such as a lot of the western and southwestern United States), you do not wish to improve alkalinity with the addition of ash into a mulch mix. But if your backyard where lands are contaminated, wood ash could be added in tiny quantities. Sprinkle handfuls around as you combine a heap.
◊ Engineered timber products: Do not include wood chips or sawdust from treated or pressure-treated timber.

Should you develop into a severe masonry enthusiast who enjoys to track and keep hot piles, then the next three things could be composted. Tracking your heap's temperature and turning it off often are crucial. Should you explain yourself as a laidback, "mulch occurs" gardening guy or woman, you are better off safe than sorry. Eliminate those problem-prone plant substances from the garbage:

◊ Weeds with seed heads. You're able to extract weeds before they go to seed and then chuck them into your compost pile as a fantastic supply of iodine. However, if seeds have the place, throw the whole plant at the garbage.
◊ Infection - or - insect-infested plant substance.
◊ Plants that propagate with invasive root systems, for example, African couch grass, Bermuda grass, bindweed, Canada thistle, and other thistles, dock marijuana, morning glory, and also others. Only a smidgen of the root substance can endure to sprout a different evening and spread havoc during your backyard.

When throwing off organic thing, however, weedy and disease-ridden sends slight guilt pangs down and up your spine, but also you do not have enough time to regularly keep a hot heap, squeezing all of the terrible things in a different bin in which it can not inadvertently be blended with all the fantastic stuff. Or place all of the terrible stuff at a significant (30- to 40-gallon), black, thick plastic garbage bag and seal it. After the amount is adequate and you've got loads of green, then nitrogen-rich substances (like grass clippings or compost) to add on it build one heap to neutralize the issues. Laboring over only one sexy pile each garden season is not as time-consuming as ensuring that each pile warms up into the red zone.
The other option is to take diseased or invasive plant substances into the regional recycling center, which collects green waste. Ask when they mulch at sufficiently substantial temperatures to ruin your issue crops. If they do, create your donation if they do not, it is straight back to Plan A.

Obtaining Your Hands on Compostable Materials

If you've got insufficient nitrogen or carbon to whip up a fantastic mixture of substances, you can wait to construct a compost pile until your landscape creates what you require, stockpiling everything you've got in the meantime. Or you can take control and move on a search for whatever you would like. You could be pleasantly surprised by the broad access to materials merely waiting for somebody to maintain them. This section provides tips on the two stockpiling what you've got and monitoring down more, in order, in the long run, you've got the very best mulch on the cube.

Stockpiling your very own organic thing

Your landscape can generate substantial quantities of substances at various times of the year. As opposed to bemoaning those fallen leaves that have to be raked in fall, contemplate them superb prosperity of carbon-rich substance that you're able to stockpile to get a calendar year's value of composting experiments. Since dry carbon substances infrequently, if ever, create bad smells, they are simple to shop. You might wish a different holding component for carbon monoxides, such as leaves, straw, sawdust, and cracked plant substance. Select up curbside plastic bags filled with leaves on your area, and heap them at an out-of-sight corner of their lawn.

Green, nitrogen-rich substance is harder to synthesize since it generally contains a higher moisture content and also may eventually become stinky and matted or bring flies. Spread grass rolls out to dry out a bit instead of leaving them into a large stack, but attempt to use them fast as their moisture is the edge in the mulch pile. A heap of new mulch loses its odor in a few weeks. Stockpile it within an out-of-the-way locale at which you can plunder it needed. In the end, should you find yourself with a heap of green garden waste in the conclusion of the year, trapping it up into compostable bits when it is new is simpler than waiting till it dries and becomes more overvalued or woody?

Rounding free organic thing

Suppose that your composting mania kicks in top gear; however, your landscape and family can not create as much organic matter as you want. Lots of complimentary organic thing requires some fantastic house! A Variety of substances and resources comprise:

◊ Free leaves: Walk around the area and see who places out bags of yard clippings or dried leaves to get garbage pickup or green waste collection. In conclusion, be aware of job crews clearing leaves in the road and gather some on your own. If local pickup fees are based on quantity, neighbors might be so delighted by the interest in composting they'll haul their luggage of leaves into your residence!

I understand and enthusiastic young teenage household whose neighbors drop bags off of trimmings in their drive on how to operate, providing a friendlier significance to the word"drive-by dumping." Express your admiration for your free organic thing by falling off a basket of hot berries or a fragrance of fresh-cut flowers from the garden. Not only can it be a neighborly gesture but also, but it also reveals real consequences of what happened to all of that"unworthy" rotting organic matter. Your contact might grow to be a home reset.

◊ Coffee reasons: Does coffee provide oxygen, but utilized grounds are tiny and moisture-laden to encourage rapid decomposition. Check with your local cafe or 24-hour restaurants nearby freeway exits. They brew umpteen baskets of coffee to maintain each of those drivers alerts!

◊ Manure: Request neighborhood farmers, stables, and dairies. Massive operations generally have pest control systems set up to take care of all that majority, which means you could be luckier with atomic operations or household farms. In urban places, assess areas called horse properties, in which taxpayers have room for a couple of horses, goats, or cows.

◊ Regional by-products: What foods or fiber products have been processed and grown in your town? Believe apple mash at wheat mills, jumps from microbreweries, grape skins in wineries, and cottonseed hulls from cotton gins.

◊ Freight shops and markets: Create branches cut and leafy veggies and veggies every day. Their in-store delis might be a supply of coffee grounds.

◊ Landscape care firms: Check out the Yellow Pages or see your local for local businesses that frequently handle trimming and mowing jobs. They cover fees to ditch clippings and trimmings in the landfill. Since they also factor at the cost of petrol, wear and tear on trucks, and worker time spent driving landfills, many are thrilled to put in a load of organic matter on your driveway. Talk about the contents together with them beforehand should you require green grass clippings or brownish leaves that are dried.

Make sure that you don't have a load of suitable plants, poisonous oleander leaves, or thorny rose bush trimmings! Additionally, talk about the chemical and pesticide fertilizers used together with the landscape manager. She could have the ability to steer the"really organic" thing for you.

◊ Utilities: Electric businesses cut trees under utility wires. They generally utilize a heavy-duty chipper/shredder, so they are a superb resource for chips. The drawback is that there is frequently a waiting list, and they might not envision a fall much ahead of time.

◊ Neighborhood municipalities: You might be blessed to reside in a neighborhood which conducts a waste-reduction job that includes dropoff/pick-up factors for the organic thing. Reduce your dried leaves fall and get a batch of mulch. Such a bargain! Check with local pest control departments, recreation, and parks providers and garden clubs, or even cooperative extension offices to locate applications in your town.

SO YOU WANT TO COMPOST?

7 WORKING WITH WORMS

Envision eating enough food daily to equal half of your weight. That is what red wiggler worms do, which makes them the ideal selection for vermicomposting.

Vermicomposting is a composting system that uses certain whale species to absorb and then convert organic matter into a beneficial soil amendment and natural fertilizer. These composting rats thrive in diverse scenarios, such as a secure indoor container that recycles your family food scraps or from complex operations made to take care of college cafeteria waste or process large amounts of animal manure from farms.

Within this chapter, I stay with all the fundamentals of an indoor family pig bin to recycle kitchen waste. It is an excellent composting method in case you don't have an outdoor garden area and wish to recycle your food scraps instead of sending them into an area or down to the garbage disposal. Even in case you've got a backyard, employing a worm composter will let you recycle cooked meals scraps that can not go on a usual compost heap.

You'll discover whatever you will need to know to begin an indoor vermicomposting program, such as descriptions of the pig species and step-by-step directions for building a bin to home them. I describe how to nourish and keep healthful worms and provide troubleshooting hints. The chapter ends with ideas for harvesting and utilizing their abundant compost.

Vermicomposting at a Nutshell

A pig's gastrointestinal tract extends the whole length of the human body. Wormfood moves through it to be excreted as castings -- a more tasteful expression for pig poop. Actual castings resemble grains of dark soil or coffee grounds. On your pig bin, castings mix with partly decomposed food bits and pig bedding to make vermicompost. It has several benefits, very similar to those of "routine" compost. When added to the soil, vermicompost enhances aeration, water retention, porosity, and parasitic action. Vermicompost additionally inhibits diseases in crops and improves plant development.

The worms aren't producing this fantastic product by themselves. The very same forms of decomposer microorganisms which operate in an outdoor compost heap will also be at work at a vermicomposting system. Worms consume germs together with pieces of plant material, so that they, too, wind up on your wealthy vermicompost.

Vermicomposting is a mesophilic procedure, meaning it happens at moderate temperatures. (Chapter 3 covers additional details on preferred temperatures ranges of composting organisms).

Worms and their helper germs create temperatures ranging from 50 to 90 degrees Fahrenheit (10 to 32 degrees Celsius). Vermicomposting is not viable in big, deep mulch piles (1 per yard [1 liter] or higher), which self-insulate and warmth up to warm or thermophilic temperature. Tons of flat surface area, approximately 8 to 12 inches (20 to 30 centimeters) deep, functions excellent for vermicomposting.

Vermicomposting has many more pros than cons. I acknowledge it might not be perfect for you if you are not fond of worms. Furthermore, if not properly handled, a vermicompost bin can entice pesky vinegar flies. However, the specialists outnumber these drawbacks and comprise the following:

◊   It takes minimal space.
◊   Apartment and condominium dwellers can compost their food scraps.
◊   It reduces the quantity of organic waste delivered to landfills.
◊   It reduces garbage set fees based on quantity.
◊   It generates a premium-quality soil change.
◊   It is an effective way to educate children about life and recycling spans.
◊   It takes very little physical labor or power.
◊   It reduces electricity and water use by eliminating the necessity to conduct in-sink trash disposal.
◊   It generates less odor and brings fewer bugs than scraps left from trash cans.

Meet with the Squirmy Stars of the Display

A considerable number of pig species exist; however, just a notable few species operate efficiently as vermicomposters. Do not purchase random worms out of bait shops or perhaps dig them from the backyard. They will not be the perfect type of heavy-duty consumers necessary to procedure kitchen waste quickly and furiously.

Composting pig species

The most commonly marketed pig for vermicomposting from the USA and Canada is that the red wiggler (Eisenia fetida). Other common names it replies to comprise brandling worm, manure worm, or even redworm. Another composting pig not as generally accessible is Eisenia Andrei, occasionally referred to as the tiger pig. In the UK, composting worms are occasionally marketed as a"combination" with a couple of species. During this period, I refer to red wigglers since they are the most typical selection for vermicomposting. Red wigglers flourish in these beautifully opulent and humid living surroundings like plantation animal manure patties or parasitic plant debris under fallen logs.

They do not tunnel into permanent or deep burrows in the earth, preferring to hang close to the surface in which the excellent rotten material is easy to get. Due to their competence at absorbing tons of organic matter and their taste for shallow dwelling quarters, they are ideal for life from shallow, family vermicomposting systems. (Watch"Hooking Up the Home and Bedding" later in this chapter for more information.)

Obtaining composting worms

Purchase from pig providers who tag their goods from genus and species (like Eisenia fetida), as opposed to common names, which differ from place to place. You do not wish to go home using worms that are not suited to this job or with possibly invasive species. Concern exists that non-native pig species, for example, Lumbricus rubellus, a European crimson pig occasionally employed for composting, could be threatening North American woods and swallowing foliage litter so quickly they're altering the nutrient cycles. Numerous animal and plant species rely upon a traditional thick mat of an organic thing that decays gradually over several decades. If the organic matter is absorbed immediately and evaporates, so will the lifeblood of this ecosystem. Even when you carefully select out live rats before dispersing vermicompost in your backyard, it is very likely to have a couple of cocoons with infants prepared to hatch and move on walkabout. Get your composting worms tagged with genus and species also assess with local specialists for queries about invasive species locally.

Request friends and co-workers for somebody who has a vermicompost bin. Joyful red wigglers within their preferred surroundings replicate frequently. Most effective vermicomposters are thrilled to"lean their herd" since overpopulation creates difficulties, as it's for every other species.

Worms are usually offered by the pound in the USA and Canada. In the U.K., they are offered by the kilo, or fractions thereof. One pound averages approximately 1,000 worms, even though the true count fluctuates based on the comparative size and age of most people. A pound of fleas is much more than plenty for the majority of families to begin.

Hooking Up the Home and Bedding

Wild composting worms reside at Mother Nature's best levels of soil and leaf litter. They do not thrive deep within the floor, as a few other parasitic species do. On your house vermicomposting program, all you need to do is replicate their favored shallow living requirements using a bin that provides a great deal of surface space (instead of proper thickness) and keep it filled up with bedding.

Red wigglers: Red wigglers, also known in their scientific names as Eisenia foetida.

How much space do your germs want?

How large of a bin you desire (and just how many worms to place inside) depends upon just how much toilet waste you need to the procedure. Review the listing of acceptable pig food in the chapter and also gauge the burden of pig food that your family generates. Weighing your kitchen bits for a week to find a rough idea can be useful.

These tips help you gauge your bin dimensions:

◊ Composting worms operate well in depths of 2 to 12 inches (20 to 30 centimeters).
◊ Supply 1 square foot (0.3 square meters) of surface area for every pound of trash to be composted. For two individuals, a bin that's two feet long by two ft full by 8 inches deep (60 x 60 x 20 centimeters) is usually adequate.
◊ Strategy on rats consuming roughly half of their weight daily: 1 lb (0.5 kilograms) of rats investigates 1/2 lb (0.2 kilograms) of scraps; two pounds (1 kilogram) of rats consume 1 lb (0.5 kilograms) of bits, etc. They could eat over that, but err on the side of caution to not hamper your bin inhabitants and make problems.

Using a brand-new vermicomposting project, it might require your rats a couple of days or weeks for up to pace, therefore take care not to overfeed them. It's simple to add more bits whenever they are plowing through your primary offerings, but it is not much interesting to get rid of excess bits or handle the issues an overload may trigger, like scents or vinegar flies.

Assembling your pig abode

Within my experience, provided that they have proper aeration, moisture, and food, worms are not worried about where they poop and eat. Bin aesthetics is an individual necessity!

In case you are considering building a house for your worms rather than purchasing a single, I suggest beginning using an easy and affordable vinyl storage bin or bins. They are offered in a lot of shapes and sizes that will agree with your worms just lovely -- you can also reuse ones which you presently have. Vinyl storage containers permit you to determine if vermicomposting matches your home with a minimum investment of money and time.

The double-decker style comprises an integrated way of harvesting vermicompost. In the event you would rather receive your feet wet with only one bin, then follow the fundamental drilling directions to the double-decker bin, then substituting an individual bin.

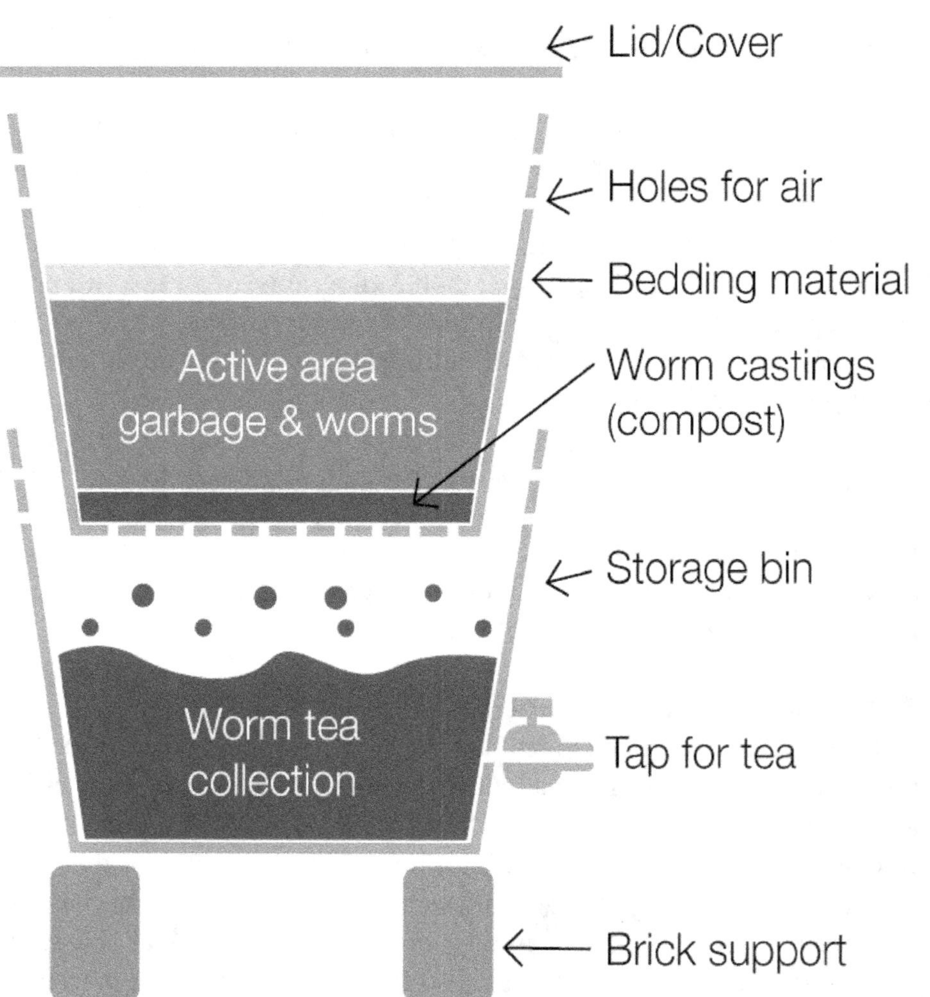

Lid/Cover
Holes for air
Bedding material
Worm castings (compost)
Active area garbage & worms
Storage bin
Worm tea collection
Tap for tea
Brick support

The substances to the double-decker pig bin comprise:

◊   Two plastic storage containers with lids. Bins must be opaque and dark since worms can not withstand light.
◊   A drill using 1/4-inch (6.35 millimeter) and also 1/16-inch (1.58 millimeter) pieces.
◊   Two bricks to place bin over ground level.

Build your bin by following these steps:

1. 1With the 1/4-inch (6.35 millimeter) drill bit, create 20 holes evenly dispersed in the base of every bin. These pockets allow drainage so states will not become too moist, and they encourage aeration, which is vital to an aerobic composting atmosphere. When it is time to crop castings, your worms may undergo the holes from 1 bin in the opposite (see Measure 5)
2. 2With the 1/16-inch (1.58 millimeter) piece, drill bigger aeration holes each 1 to 2 inches (2.5 to 5 centimeters) on every side of every bin near top border.
3. Utilizing the 1/16-inch (1.58 millimeter) piece, drill around 30 little holes at the front of one of those pliers to permit aeration. Leave the next lid to function as a tray to catch drips.
4. Put the drip tray onto the ground. Position the two bricks onto the tray to supply decent equilibrium when a single full bin is put on top. Raising the pig bin a few inches away from the ground with bricks encourages airflow under it.
5. Insert the next bin once you are all set to crop completed vermicompost (see the section"Slow harvest process" later in the chapter for directions).

Choosing a fabricated worm bin

Improved curiosity about vermicomposting is represented by a rise in the wide variety of fabricated worm bins out there in the past couple of decades. A fabricated bin will probably cost you a little more than recycling a free plastic storage container (see the previous section for directions). Bins can vary in cost from $50 to $175.

Within their healthy surroundings, composting worms reside at or close to the ground surface. They do not dip deep into the floor, so plenty of shallow surface region is much more significant than a container. That is why most fabricated worm bins have been created with some design of numerous, shallow piling shelves. They provide greater surface area inside the unit's entire relatively modest footprint.

Practice the sooner tips under"Building your worm abode" for estimating the sum of your kitchen scraps as well as the number of worms you will have to eat it. Compare it to the producer's specifications to the number of worms per given merchandise homes or just how much kitchen waste it will hold to obtain the most acceptable size.

Stacked layouts make it possible for rats to do what comes naturally: proceed upwards to seek out food. Start worms with food and bedding at the base tray. As soon as they finish off that department, provide food and bedding within another tray, and upward they will proceed, leaving vermicompost supporting to heal till you crop it. Some pig bins have spigots to drain fluid. But, the liquid that flows from the base of a worm bin isn't vermicomposted tea. It is leachate or surplus liquid, which flows through the fundamental issue. As it's an infusion of undigested substances, it can include pathogens dangerous to crops. Authentic vermicompost tea is produced from means of finished (digested) vermicompost from the plain water.

Making the bed

Offer moist bedding in any way times to the worms to romp about in while they process your fundamental issue. They've no guts or gills and breathe through their skin, and that they were coated with mucous. Dissolved oxygen enters through their skin to the blood. Worms must reside in moist, humid environments because when their skin dries out, then they perish.

As time passes, rats have their bedding alongside your food scraps, but that is fine. By then, you are going to be prepared to harvest castings and supply bedding. Getting bedding to your worms requires just two substances: 2 handfuls of indigenous soil and paper or computer newspaper. You might also utilize leaves and shredded cardboard for bedding, possibly instead of paper or along with it. I favor paper since there's always a lot of it to be recycled, and it's simple to utilize.

Follow the following steps to create your worms exactly the Kind of bedding they will never want to leave:

1. Wash bins thoroughly before including worms and bedding.
2. Tear paper to 1-inch (2.5-centimeter) strips. Fill one side of your sink. Soak the paper in it. Lift it out and then allow excess water drain from the opposing side of this sink. Do not squeeze the paper since then it can dry to hard balls.
3. Gently put the paper from the bin. Composting worms operate in 8 to 12 inches (20 to 30 centimeters) of bedding thickness. Fill out the bin at least 12 inches (30 centimeters) deep since the bedding will repay somewhat. Fluff up the bed that it's loose, together with air pockets, instead of compacted.
4. Sprinkle two handfuls of the native soil to the bed. It gives endurance for the worms' digestive process and adds germs to assist with decomposition.
5. Bury 1 couple of food scraps from the bed. Do not overpower red wigglers with an excessive amount of food in the very first week while they are getting acclimated. Whenever these bits are gone and add more, slowly working up to more significant amounts. (The following section clarifies what worms like to consume.)

Introducing worms for their new residence

Set your red wigglers in addition to the moist bedding, plus they will start evaporating into it. Should they look slow to proceed, glow a bright light over the bin? They should dip for the darkened depths. Chow Time! Feeding Your Worms Vermicomposting worms on your indoor bin consume precisely the exact organic goodies which you add into an outside compost pile, such as spent garden crops, landscape trimmings, scrap paper, and kitchen scraps. But, I suppose you'll feed them kitchen bits.

Gently split your bin to"zones" and salty food scraps in various portions of the bin together with every feeding. Strategy feeding your worms around half of their weight in food scraps every day. When beginning a new bin, then provide only a small number of meals until they get acclimated and begin digging into your requirements. As a general principle, nourish your worms once the vast majority of the other food has vanished.

What is on the menu

Even the greater variety in components, the higher your vermicompost. Try not to overload your worm bin using vegetable and fruit skins, which might bring vinegar flies.

Additionally, avoid a lot of salty food waste that will dry from the harmful little worms. Everything in moderation!

Worms have been proven to get food tastes (actually), so experiment to find out precisely what exactly your red wigglers prefer. Here is a hint: candy mushy things like melon, pumpkin, and squash is a favorite in my property. Other Fantastic developments include

◊   Raw or cooked veggies
◊   Coffee grounds and filters
◊   Tea and newspaper bags
◊   Stale bread and grain products
◊   Ground-up eggshells
◊   Fruit rinds and cores

Insert citrus in rather little quantities; therefore, the bin does not become overly acidic. (See the section"pH amounts" later in the chapter for additional information.)

Place apple cores on your worm bin. They will have worms sticking from these, exactly enjoy the drawings in children's publications. Children think that is a hoot!

Just as there are things Which Shouldn't be added into a routine compost pile, These items are not proper pig meals:

◊   Fish, poultry, or milk: All these foodstuffs can turn rancid and pungent because they decompose, and draw undesirables like houseflies or vinegar flies (also referred to as fruit flies).
◊   Greases and oils: Worms breathe through their skin. Oils and dirt coating their skin and stop them from breathing.
◊   Pet or human waste: It could include pathogens that can be transmitted to people.

To chop or not to chop (again)

Chopping bits to two - to 4-inch (5- on 10-centimeter) pieces speeds the decomposition procedure on your vermicomposting bin, then as it can on the external compost heap. But, it is not always necessary if you're in a rush and your bin was working well. Worms can do with remarkable alacrity on big chunks of food waste. I plunked a half dozen cantaloupe in my bin upside down without paring -- grated pulp, flesh, rind, and all. Within two weeks, my Wormingtons stripped down it into some paper-thin sheet of the rind, which exhibited a fragile ribbed pattern once I held it up into the light. Efficient little creatures, these red wigglers.

Maintaining Your Worms' Comfort Zone

Along with food and bedding, worms require proper temperature, oxygen, moisture, and pH levels to flourish. Plus, they do not enjoy the lights left!

Light

Worms do not have eyes, but they are still incredibly sensitive to light and proceed away from bright lighting whenever they could. If subjected to bright light for one hour, a few rats become paralyzed. Not able to go off, they dry out and perish. Set your bin at a dark place, keep a lid on to toss out a towel or other covering it over to block lighting.

Temperature

The best temperature range for red wigglers is from 55 to 77 degrees Fahrenheit (13 to 25 degrees Celsius). You're able to stretch these constraints by 50 to 84 degrees Fahrenheit (10 to 29 degrees Celsius), but they might not act as much organic matter or replicate as vigorously.

Moisture

Maintaining wet bedding is essential. Worm bedding needs to be 60 to 85% humidity. Based on what sorts of food scraps that you provide, the bedding can stay moist. However, I've always needed to include moisture from misting with a water spray bottle or drizzle drops of water throughout the mattress occasionally. On the flip side, do not allow the bin to turn into a swamp. Wet conditions flip the bin to some bronchial vascular composting system. (In case you read Chapter 4, then you are aware that anaerobic composting is stinky!) Worms have to stay at a moist, humid environment in any way times, or else they will perish.

Breathing room

Crimson wigglers require oxygen to keep their home within an aerobic (with air), sweet-smelling system. Be mindful not to let bedding to become overly wet or to include an excessive amount of food at the same time, which might deplete oxygen levels. After per week or so, aerate the bedding gently fluffing it up. If you are thinking about worms, use rubber gloves, or use a considerable plastic spoon or spatula to lift and twist.

PH levels

pH is an indicator of acidity and alkalinity on a scale from 1 to 14. Acidic is just 1 to 6; g is to 14; 7 is neutral. In temperament, rats live in a variety of pH levels, and however, at the little space of the bin, it is ideal for maintaining pH in the assortment of 6.8 to 7.2.

Doesn't imply you need to measure pH levels? Not unless you would like to. I don't assess the pH level in a worm bin. I guess it if you experience difficulties, and much more apparent troubleshooting approaches do not fix them. The next food alterations can help you keep pH levels that don't skip from whack:

◊   Limit the number of citrus bits to stop the bin from becoming too acidic.
◊   Insert crushed eggshells to reduce acidity.
◊   Restrict the number of nitrogen-rich substances that quickly decompose, like a wealth of coffee grounds. Nitrogen substances release ammonia and boost pH levels.

In case you are interested in analyzing the pH of the worm bin, backyard shops and internet retailers sell different styles of easy pH testing kits, like paper strands, capsules, or yards. Although not necessarily tremendously precise, they will supply you with a troubleshooting manual.

Tackling issues with Your Own Worm Bin

If you abide by the tips in this chapter, then your vermicomposting attempts ought to be prosperous. But only in case you face difficulties.

Odor

Most probably, the bedding is moist and compacted along with your own aerobic (with air) vermicomposting surgery is becoming anaerobic (without air). Chapter 4 explains the anaerobic decomposers since the germs which give away stinky gas as a byproduct in the exertions. If conditions are not too bad, you might have the ability to combine warm bedding to warm up extra moisture. If the bedding is a shameful, icky mess, then salvage the worms, then wash out the bin, and then begin anew with new bedding.

Mites

As Chapter 3 explains, mites are a part of this extensive system of decomposer organisms, and tiny populations of fleas are typical in both vermicomposting systems. But if mite inhabitants leap from control, they can become poisonous to your own worms' wellbeing. The perfect approach to avert a mite issue would be to take decent care of the pig bin, supplying proper aeration, moisture, and meals. Too moist beds, the overabundance of foods, and foods with higher moisture content all of prefer mites.

Dying worms

Worm bodies are made mainly of water. When rats die, you are not likely to detect any pig carcasses because they decompose so fast.

But if you see a lot of dead fleas at one time, it is time to inquire into the reason. It is probably best to crop healthy worms, scrub the bin out, and begin with new bedding.

What Worms Contribute for Your Compost: The squirrel's Telephone

Castings are the substances that have traveled throughout the worms' digestive processes and emerge the other end since excrement. Castings resemble dark pieces of dirt or coffee grounds. Integrated using all the castings will be pieces of bedding and food scraps, which are more or less decomposed worms, and also possibly worm cocoons holding infants. The whole combination is known as vermicompost.

As your outside compost heap shrinks in size with time, thus does the rats' bedding. It becomes even darker in color, unrecognizable because of its first material, and much more"compost-like." Castings also collect from the bin, that produces a hazardous environment for its red wigglers. Consider it. They are living in feces. That can not go on forever; therefore, you must harvest the vermicompost and prepare for new bedding.

For a principle, change the bedding and also crop castings each four to six weeks. Your bin might endure for a few weeks without harvesting, however, if you are first gaining expertise, track your bin for indications that life will be stressful, like the pig population decreasing, food evaporating less fast, or a lack of cocoons with infants along the road. If these circumstances exist, it is time to crop your vermicompost (see the following section) and offer to bed.

Harvesting vermicompost

During this section, I provide you two ways of reaping vermicompost. One method relies upon the worms' want to consume; another benefit from the dislike of bright light.

When picking vermicompost, you will detect shiny, yellow to light brownish constructions shaped like 1/8-inch-long grape seeds, even together with a single pointy end and another round. All these are parasitic cocoons, holding two to 20 infant worms per day. Transfer cocoons into the brand new bin with all the worms.

Slow crop strategy

This way of harvesting vermicompost is much more passive on your character than the rapid harvest strategy I pay in the next part. Here, you mostly await the worms to proceed toward the meals. Follow the following steps to your slow harvest process together with your doubledecker bins:

1. When you are ready to crop castings in the very first bin, put fresh damp bedding material from the next bin.
2. Remove the lid in the very first bin, and then place the bin right on the vermicompost face of the bin. Set the lid onto the brand new bin.
3. Bury all of the fresh food scraps from the brand new bin. Gradually, many worms will relocate into the brand new bin seeking food since it is their nature to go into the surface to nourish. This can take two to three months (or perhaps longer). Poke around in the bins occasionally to track their activity.
4. After most rats have reached the movement, crop vermicompost in the very first bin.
5. Eliminate any lingering worms and set them in the next bin.

If you decide to vermicompost with one bin, then precisely the identical principle of harvesting employs: Worms go for the line, therefore place food scraps onto a single side of this bin. Once they have traveled to the side, crop the vacated vermicompost, then replicate the procedure on the opposing side.

Quick crop strategy

Together with the rapid harvest process, you, umm, invite your worms to find a go on by dumping them from the bin and to the light. Their typical aversion to light functions in your favor. Follow the following steps to use the fast Way of harvesting vermicompost:

1. Distribute a plastic sheeting or old shower curtain in which it could remain conveniently for many hours at bright lighting -- either sun or artificial lighting.
2. Dump the entire contents of the bin on the tarp at a pyramid-shaped heap (broad at the bottom, peaked in the top). Worms in the very top and outer borders start diving to the mulch depths to escape in the light.
3. While waiting for your worms to get a pass on, wash their bin using new, moist bedding (see the prior section"Creating the mattress" for bedding directions). Bury about half of the food scraps you generally supply. Even the upheaval of a move is more stressful, therefore let them fix instead of overfeeding.
4. After 15 to 30 minutes, then lightly scrape off the upper levels of vermicompost, which needs to be mainly worm-free. Pick any stragglers, and then transfer them into the bin. Reshape the volcano. Wait around for many more worms to dip to the depths.
5. Repeat this procedure as many times as required until you get to the bottom of this pyramid. Now, it is going to be mainly bulk of red wigglers, which you can get and transfer into the bin.

Recall pig bodies need to remain moist so that they could breathe, or else they will perish. Make sure that you don't overlook these in harsh lighting. Set your kitchen or watch timer to ring every quarter-hour. If picking outside, track the heap to fend off some plundering birds.

Utilizing vermicompost

Wealthy vermicompost is much wanted by accomplished anglers and plant shelters. Though the actual nutrient content of vermicompost fluctuates based on the kinds of bedding and food the rats consume, evaluations demonstrate that vermicompost includes 5 to 11 times greater magnesium, calcium, phosphorus, potassium, and potassium compared to plain soil. These nutrients bring about healthy plant development.

Castings give beneficial microbial action that combats plant disorder, and they feature growth hormones that encourage seed germination. Castings are lightweight, virtually indestructible. Once added to soil as an alteration, castings enhance aeration and water-holding capacity.

Vermicompost may be implemented in precisely the very same approaches you use finished compost out of a standard outside the composting system, like mulching around plants, top-dressing yards, or mixing it into flower and vegetable beds. If first amounts are restricted, utilize your vermicompost into top-dress your favorite houseplants or place it to use in which you're able to optimize its advantages, like adding it into soil mixture for container crops. Eliminate any worms or cocoons, since the living conditions in containers are not suited to them.

8   ADDING COVER CROPS AND MANURES

Regardless of their title, cover crops are not grown to crop for animal or human consumption, such as other plants. Instead, they are planted to defend the soil and enhance its quality. If you are only getting underway with homemade attempts or you do not have enough organic matter to create compost to fulfill all of your gardening requirements, think about placing a cover crop for a means to better the soil or to generate composting ingredients.

Within this chapter, I specify the small gap between a cover crop along with its green manure cousin, and then I pay the several advantages they provide to improve your soil-building jobs. Finally, they direct you to a much healthier, more productive backyard, supplying precisely the very same perks you would achieve by adding mulch. Besides, I provide recommendations about which and when to plant from a geographical region, also I contain instructions for integrating the plants into your soil, essentially letting them mulch in place.

Recognizing the worth of Cover Crops and Green Manures

Cover crop and green components are conditions that frequently are used responsibly. Precisely the identical plant options have been developed for either function, and they supply long, similar lists of developments to your soil. To simplify things, I use the expression"cover crop" during this phase, but here is an explanation of the marginally different usages:

◊   Cover plants are usually sown to stop soil erosion and inhibit weed growth if your backyard place is left unplanted through its dormant period. "Covering" the dirt with plants reduces erosion from rain, wind, and snowmelt. Crop follicles hang on dirt particles, holding precious topsoil in place.

◊   Green manures are usually sown to boost oxygen availability and add organic matter into the soil throughout the growing season.

Though those small differences in definition exist, in practice, the identical plant species might be grown as a cover crop or a green mulch. In the rest of the section, I explain the several benefits cover plants bring to their own home and soil-building pursuits.

Preventing erosion

It might occur more slowly than you be aware of this; however, the blend of wind and runoff from rain and snowmelt gradually erodes your backyard's topsoil -- that harbors crucial nutrients and organic matter. A cover crop's aboveground foliage buffers dirt against the constant ravages of water and wind, whereas underground roots perform their part to decrease erosion by holding soil particles in place. Since climate change has been attracting more intense weather conditions, it is possible to help stop soil erosion by planting a cover crop as soon as your backyard is located fallow through its dormant period.

Adding organic matter

Organic matter improves soil fertility and structure. Chapter 3 explains the continuing work of countless organisms decomposing organic matter on your mulch pile. The very same animals are functioning on your soil, reducing natural debris to usable pieces of nourishment for crops and other animals to consume.

It is your choice to replenish organic matter and nutrients on your backyard soil to deliver a continuous fuel supply for these animals. Another option is to plant a cover crop right on your backyard ahead of your planting period. Cover plants perform a function much like that of germ, providing sterile organic things for a plethora of germs, fungi, viruses, and other soil organisms to construct a booming soil food web.

Decreasing soil compaction

Cover plants inhibit rain from tapping on the bare floor, which disrupts the ground's natural feel and triggers compaction. As time passes, compacted dirt surfaces clog, impeding water retention along with easing runoff. Along with boosting soil erosion, water runoff carries nutrients away and might leach toxic or undesirable chemicals into groundwater sources.

Improving tilth

The large, fibrous root systems of several cover plants (notably grasses and grains) permeate widely throughout the ground, making elaborate paths for successful water and air infiltration. It consequently improves tilth, which describes the soil's physical capability to encourage plant growth. Soil with good tilth is tight, crumbly, and simple for you to dig and utilize. Deep-rooted plants are especially helpful for enhancing clay or silty soils.

Building and including nitrogen

Nitrogen is one of the three crucial elements which plants need to flourish. (Both are potassium and phosphorus.) Nitrogen is currently in limited distribution in most lands, and even when you're blessed to the backyard where lands are muddy, nitrogen is going to be emptied with recurrent growing cycles in case you do not replenish it with fertilizer or mulch.

Planting a legume cover crop that will be capable of creating its own immune additionally enhances nitrogen availability in your backyard. (Read more about the following in the chapter in the area"Legumes" and in the faucet" Fixating.")

Feeding valuable insects

Cover plants provide food and habitat (in the kind of pollen and nectar) for valuable pollinators, like bees. With bees, mealtime is utterly dull since these unique creatures are responsible for devoting one-third of those food plants which you and I eat. Cover crops also encourage a multitude of valuable predators, such as lady beetles, parasitic wasps, predatory mites, and spiders. They serve important biological control agents to maintain insect populations in check without forcing you to resort to chemical pesticides.

Inhibiting bud expansion

Cover plants are occasionally known as"living mulch" due to the capacity to out-compete weeds. As a layer of mulch spread in addition to the dirt deters weeds, a compact cover crop inhibits weeds by shading the ground. When the sun is obstructed, weed seeds can not germinate. Additionally, a thick cover harvest out-competes present weeds for sunshine, water, and atmosphere. If you are trying hard to acquire bud plants under management (maybe a prior owner of your house let things escape hands), plant a living mulch cover crop between rows on the garden or orchard.

Surveying Your Cover Crop Choices

Cover plants split into three groups: seeds, legumes, and also a catch-all"other" class. These plants can be annuals, which germinate, grow, plant, and die in 1 season, or else they might be more perennials, that reside for several decades, though they usually go dormant on your area's off-season. Regardless of group, cover plants display some combination of these attributes, making them quite competent in their occupation:

◊ Grow fast to supply significant organic thing to add into the soil or mulch heap
◊ Create fibrous root systems which spread through dirt
◊ Are comparatively simple to reduce or mow and integrate into the dirt or contribute to the compost pile
◊ Insert nitrogen

Legume cover crops include more nitrogen to the land, whereas marijuana cover plants do a much better job of raising the whole organic issue. Sowing a cover crop that includes both the legume and a bud supplies you with the very best of the two.

Lots of cover plants are workhorses that take a wide selection of growing conditions. Temperature is generally the limiting factor since some will not endure cold or withstand intense heat. For your fast path to figuring out that insure crop to plant, get in touch with a full-size backyard nursery or your closest farm supply shop for a fast and effortless reply to your cover harvest conundrum. (Even most metropolitan regions have a farm supply shop or 2.) Staff may advise you on what works in your area, and they can likely find it on their shelves, also.

Legumes

Legumes are plants that make a bean or pea pod. Frequent beans in landscapes or gardens you could already grow to comprise French, runner, or snap beans, legumes, aromatic sweet pea blossoms, acacia trees, along with mesquite trees, to mention only a couple of Cover crop beans contain alfalfa, beans, clovers, peas, and trefoil.

Legume plants possess a symbiotic relationship with Rhizobia bacteria, where they unite attempts to convert nitrogen from the atmosphere to a form of nitrogen that plant roots can absorb from the dirt. This conversion process is known as nitrogen fixation (see the sidebar" Fixating on nitrogen" for longer).

Grasses

Unlike beans, grasses (a class which includes cereal grains, like oats) aren't capable of nitrogen fixation, even though they do include lots of organic matter into your ground when trimming and turned beneath. Their reproductive and matting root programs additionally inhibit soil erosion. Cover crops within this class include yearly (Italian) or perennial ryegrass, Sudangrass, cereal, cheese, grazing or winter rye (that is not precisely the like ryegrass), along with corn)

Other protect plants

Neither legume nor bud, buckwheat is a superb cover crop should you want a fast-grower into out-compete weeds. It evolves in 30 to 45 days in hot weather. Buckwheat tolerates low-fertility dirt and thrives in hot temperatures. Other protect plants that fall to this catchall group are cabbage-family plants like kale and mustard, fenugreek, and phacelia.

Planting and Turning Over Cover Crops

General features of geographical gardening areas dictate when you need to plant cover plants. This section provides guidelines for various sowing seasons, and so that I also provide you directions for finally integrating your cover crop into the ground for decomposition (another fantastic kind of composting!).

Sowing seasons

As to plant crops, plants are based on part on your own area's gardening seasons in addition to about what you wish to reach using a cover crop. Have you been protecting the soil from erosion throughout your region's spring rainy day? If this is so, plant in autumn so that plants are up and running. Would you need to put in a fast burst of nutrients into the ground before beginning a fresh summer backyard? If that's the case, sow crops whenever you can following your last frost date. This information provides you with planting schedules according to overall gardening and temperature seasons. Check to your favorite garden center, farm supply shop, or a county cooperative extension office to fine-tune your planting period.

◊ Cold or snowy winters with a single brief summer climbing season: Planting period: August to late September. (Option planting interval: Following your place's last frost in spring) Sow cover plants in time for four weeks of development before chilly weather halts growth. Plants reverted together with the final of those warm soil temperatures and also created leaves to protect soil from erosion during winter. When temperatures warm in spring, the expansion of perennial plants will restart. If you are waiting for optimum harvesting time for vegetable plants still producing on your backyard, you might sow cover crops between rows or "intercrop" round the borders of vegetable plants

◊ Somewhat moderate temperatures or rainy winters using a longer growing up; many households dormant in winter planting span: August through early December (Alternative planting interval: Following your region's last frost in spring.) The sooner the sowing, the higher recognized the cover crop would probably be since most seeds do not germinate well in cold or wet soils.

◊ Hot or warm summers using two gardening seasons or yearlong gardening: Planting interval: May through June. (Option planting period: Before gardening period.) The sooner you sow seeds better, permitting your cover harvest to set until extreme heat arrives. Late sowings need further moisture to get plants off to a fantastic start.

Implementing your old cover harvest into the ground

As a general principle, cut and integrate cover crops to the ground at least a couple of weeks before placing your next garden to permit some decomposition to happen.

Benefits attained out of your cover harvest depend on the length of time your crop is allowed to grow until you cut and flip it under. As a general principle, enable plants to develop for as long as you can optimize organic mass without creating woody stems or seed thoughts. Mature plant issues having tough or woody stalks are harder physically that you mow or cut and combine within the ground. Additionally, it includes higher amounts of carbon, and that land microorganisms divide more gradually concerning nitrogen. (Switch back to Chapter 3 for a summary of their favored eating customs of decomposer organisms)

Once ready to crop, chop or throw down the foliage, then shred or split it into smaller sections for faster decomposition. If you would like to plant fast, the bigger the portions, the lumpy and bumpy your dirt will be. If you are in no rush to plant, then more significant bits are not as an issue.

Function the organic matter into the upper layer of dirt, utilizing a dirt branch, shovel, or spade. (The heavier it is integrated, the lower the decomposition speed.) Rototilling is yet another option for incorporating sterile, rough plant material. If harvesting in spring, then reduce cover plants if your typical daily soil temperature strikes 55 degrees Fahrenheit (13 degrees Celsius). That is when enormous populations of soil creatures begin gearing up to the decomposition procedure.

The subsequent sections offer additional hints for timing your crop according to your target to your soil.

Target: Reduce the decomposition rate so nutrients can be found whenever possible on the next lawn as soon as harvest: Cut your harvest when crops have complete vegetative cover, however before blossoms look.

Brand New, moisture-rich foliage promotes a fast spike in soil microbial action, which leads to rapid decomposition of organic matter and discharge of nourishment Level of difficulty: This is the most straightforward stage that you cut and integrate plant matter to the ground by hand.

Target: collect whole organic thing When to harvest: Cut before plants reach full bloom or any time they are in full blossom.

Permit plants to grow as much organic matter (scientists predict that biomass) as possible before generating seeds. This period helps encourage the continuous decomposition of organic substances and discharge of nutrients to the soil within a longer time than another option.

Level of issue: Coarser plant issue is much more challenging to include by hand.

Target: collect dirt aeration and decrease compaction When to harvest: Cut after blossom but before seeds set. Longlasting root programs and woody, rough plant issue enhances aeration throughout the ground.

Level of difficulty: You are very likely to desire some rototiller or other energy equipment to integrate woody substance into the ground (check the subsequent section "To whether or not to until").

The period is catchy should you wait to include cover crops following disagreeable endings. Make sure you reduce plants and use them before they plant. If permitted to go to seed, then you might have cover plants reappearing for a long time to vex you! Buckwheat and hairy vetch might become invasive if permitted to go to seed.

Target: Grow green thing to grow your compost pile When to harvest: Cut before plants reach full bloom or any time they are in full blossom. Add leaves to a compost pile for a source of iodine. Let the bottoms of these plants to die in position or integrate into the soil to add organic matter. When eliminating the nitrogen-rich green foliage, then realize those insure plants absorbed valuable nutrients out of the soil, which has to be replenished with some combo of fertilizer and compost before planting your garden.

Degree of problem: This is an effortless stage that you cut foliage to grow compost.

To till or not to until

Tilling (also referred to as rotary-tilling, rototilling(or rotovating) using gear is a labor-saving technique to integrate organic matter in the own cover crops into the ground. The blades or tines of this tiller slit through the upper 6 to 12 inches (15 to 30 centimeters) of dirt, mixing and chopping uniformly. But, tilling additionally causes harmful impacts to a soil's ecosystem as well as construction. It kills beneficial soil organisms, like earthworms. Overfilling pulverizes dirt particles and hurts soil structure, which consequently inhibits aeration and drainage and also promotes compaction and erosion.

If your objective is to construct soil construction teeming with parasitic life (that is a significant advantage of planting cover crops), then you might choose to limit tilling using gear and then turn the dirt and incorporate organic things by hand using a dirt fork or spade. (It is excellent exercise and really kind of relaxing if you get into a rhythm)

For more significant regions where hand-turning is not possible, limit the general quantity of tilling. It's not vital to emphasize and pulverize everything into salt-sized pieces, which destroys soil structure. Maintaining nearly all the natural residue at the top couple inches of dirt promotes microbial action, so attempt to avoid tilling also intensely. At length, never operate with or walk to moist dirt, which compacts it, decreasing water and air penetration.

Should you like to become a no-till gardener, then take a look at another chapter for one more option. It ensures a dirt construction method that needs no digging in your part. Instead, just spread organic matter onto the ground to decompose in position.

9 COMPOSTING IN SHEETS

Sheet composting is a way of improving your soil by adding organic matter. Rather than creating a compost pile or even filling a bin or trench, you disperse your organic matter in addition to the ground in sheets, in which it could decompose where you require it. Within this chapter, I pay the benefits and pitfalls of sheet composting and describe how to perform it. I end with an illustration of producing garden beds using a version of the sheet in which plants grow inside layers of organic matter.

Sheet Composting: Read All About It

Sheet composting can remind one of the additional soil-improvement procedures, such as using a layer of compost mulch for a top-dressing. The distinction is that you just need sheet mulch to decompose quickly instead of stay in place to safeguard the soil with time. Since sheet composting offers organic matter and nutrients into the ground, it might be thought of as a variant of a cover crop. Unlike a cover crop, however, sheet mulch does not need to be boiled at the end of its life cycle -- it is already dead and decomposing!

Pros and cons

Sheet composting is well worth considering if you're on the lookout for a different means to compost and improve soil quality. This procedure has its benefits and disadvantages; however, it is well worth noting the prospective problems I summarize in this segment are rather simple to prevent or fix.

As you determine how long and labor to expend any compost pile you assemble, you determine how much effort to put money into sheet soil. And the same as a compost pile, the more significant upfront effort you spend, the faster the decomposition speed. A fantastic benefit of the sheet is the fact that it is perfectly fine for active gardeners to disperse materials since they have been and walk off to allow them gradually decompose over time. As an alternative, you might incur a bit more labor pruning organic matter into smaller portions before dispersing. You could also opt to turn your coating of sheet mulch below the soil. These last two activities hasten the decomposition procedure.

Though it's initially straightforward to begin, sheet composting has a couple of drawbacks that need a small amount of additional work to conquer. Materials can be slow to decompose compared to your compost pile with adequate size to make hospitable requirements for its decomposer organisms, which do the majority of the job. But if you are progressing a brand new region and in no specific rush, slow decomposition is a simple path to enhanced soil for prospective garden beds.

Another possible issue with sheet composting is those robust decomposer organisms said above may rob the land of available nitrogen resources since they divide carbon substances in the sheet mulch coating, leaving inadequate nitrogen reserves in the dirt to neighboring plants to consume. This result is known as nitrogen immobilization. Decomposers maintain nitrogen in their bodies and recycle it as they replicate and die (and eat every other) before the rotting of the sheet mulch is nearing a conclusion. Then, nearly all organisms die, discharging nitrogen stored inside their bodies for plant roots to absorb. To make sure that your plants do not go thirsty for nitrogen, then let a minimum of one full up to a year for decomposition to happen before planting.

In case you've got thick layers of moist, nitrogen-rich substances (for example, fresh grass clippings or manure), maintain the method of turning and rancid by turning these kinds of substances under the ground or intermixing them with layers of warm, brown substances.

If you decide to sheet mulch kitchen scraps or food waste, then turn it below the dirt for quicker decomposition and also to discourage pests. After turning food pieces beneath, spread another layer of non-kitchen garbage stuff in addition to the ground, like dried leaves or straw. Other options for composting kitchen scraps comprise trench composting (see Chapter 4) or utilizing pest-proof bins (see Chapter 5).

Ultimately, the procedure for sheet composting does not achieve satisfactorily hot temperatures to destroy weed seeds or plant compounds. (Therefore, sheet composting is occasionally known as a"chilly" method.) Make sure you remove any of these undesirables before dispersing organic substances as sheet compost

Sheet Mulching from the Ground Up

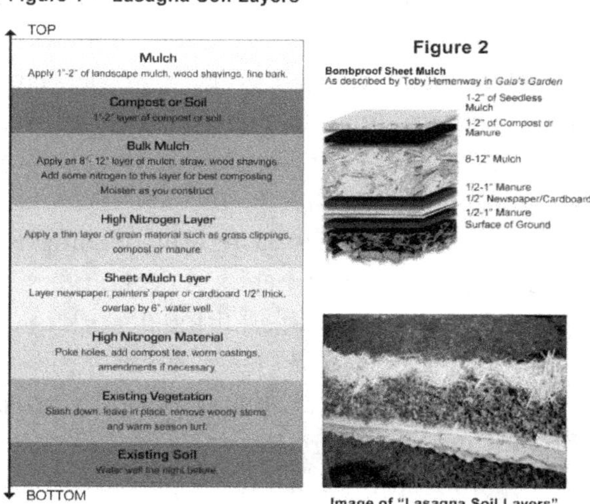

Where and when to put sheets of compost.

A fantastic place for sheet composting is an area where you'd love to develop a brand new garden finally. Distribute layers of sheet mulch and receive a jump-start on land enrichment. Other great candidates for sheet composting are modern garden beds; you don't mind letting go fallow (unplanted) for 3 to 12 weeks.

Strategy in your sheet compost carrying a full year and up to a year to decompose until you replant. The actual time involved is based upon the kind of organic thing you distribute, the depth of this coating of organic things, and also just how much preparation work you decide to do.

When to disperse sheet compost is dependent upon your growing area and timeframe for planting. If you are sheet composting to initiate a new mattress in a couple of years, timing is not essential, and you may simply layer stuff whenever you have them.

If you are sheet straightened beneath a current garden, employ organic things when you have pulled spent crops after your growing year. Organic substances can decompose through the dormant period when you aren't developing anything, anyhow. So long as the invested crops that you pull are not infested with insects or diseases, it is possible to throw them in addition to the dirt as a portion of the sheet Candles components.

In areas with warm summers and yearlong growing, sheet mulch is usually dispersed in the conclusion of spring gardening. Decomposition happens over the summertime, and you are all set to replant when temperatures abate from the autumn. But, decomposition might be slow in case of substances dry, and summer storms are lean. You might have to occasionally sprinkle water on your sheet mulch to help keep the process moving.

In areas where summer is the primary growing season, coating sheet mulch in autumn allows it to decompose during winter months, or spring and winter. You are going to be prepared to prepare soil and plant in spring or summer, depending upon the regional conditions and how quickly material decomposes. Another option is to employ sheet mulch on the summer (presuming you do not wish to plant) and allow it to decompose before the next spring.

Getting down to components

Utilize precisely the very same kinds of organic things for sheet composting, which you would add to your compost piles, such as the two spoonfuls, including dried leaves, cardboard, and soybeans, and greens, like grass clippings and garden plants that are spent.

Even new weeds could be dragged and used as greens, even provided that they do not have spread or seeds from invasive root runners who endure infiltrating your backyard. But, let different weeds wilt thoroughly before adding these to be confident they don't grow and survive. If you would like to accelerate the decomposition procedure for sheet pruning, block or shred organic matter to little pieces before dispersing it. The bigger the first parts of organic matter, the greater surface area can be found to the decomposer organisms. Additionally, integrating your sheet mulch layer beneath the top couple inches of dirt once you disperse it hastens decomposition. You can achieve so by hand using a dirt fork or shovel, or utilize a rototiller.

Utilize one of the following approaches, based on the components You Decide to integrate on your sheet ammunition:

◊ Employ about two to eight inches (5 to 20 centimeters) of natural material over the region to decompose in place as can be. When you are prepared to plant another time, then turn the stays of this organic matter below.

◊ If you've just moist, compacted materials high in nitrogen, like fresh grass clippings or manure, use in a thin layer (1 to 3 inches, or 2.5 to 2 centimeters). Then turn it beneath to accelerate decomposition and decrease odor possible. Alternately, blend in moist, heavy materials using warm, loose carbon substances, such as leaves or straw.

Sheet Composting and Gardening at One Measure

Spreading layers of organic matter in addition to the ground as sheet mulch will call to mind exactly what you observe walking across a path through the forests. Mother Nature stacks up a wealth of natural debris leaves, pine needles, fallen trees, animal waste, plus far more. Moistened occasionally by snow and rain, churned by the end, and absorbed from decomposer organisms, all of this debris slowly transforms into re humus. (Chapter 1 explains this excellent final product of decomposition.) Surprisingly varied vegetation sprouts and grew within this surface of a nutrient-rich rotted organic thing. This section describes how to replicate that procedure in your backyard.

Mimicking Mother Nature's demonstrated techniques is precisely what permaculture is about. Quite simply said, permaculture is a method of copying and observing nature to lessen people's harmful effects on Earth. It intends to incorporate human needs for food and shelter using an area's existing intertwined relationships of plants, animals, soils, and climate variations.

Building garden soil

Permaculture principles offer you diverse techniques based upon your demands and regional attributes.

However, the next soil-building process adapted from permaculture approaches operates in which you ship and provides a simple introduction to working together with and profiting from natural methods:

1. Eliminate or cut some current vegetation to the floor, and then rake the area smooth.
2. Stir organic nitrogen contamination, like alfalfa meal or cottonseed meal, to pay the region. Follow recommendations about the packing for numbers to employ.
3. Blood meal and fish meal can also be organic nitrogen resources. But, their aromas, though not too noticeable to people, may bring in pests, such as dogs that dig glee to obtain the source.
4. Twist 6 inches (15 centimeters) of compost or plants in addition to the nitrogen.
5. Fresh mulch develops a"hot" zone because it decomposes, which might burn plant roots. If just new manure can be obtained, wait at least two weeks to sow seeds or transplant seedlings into the mixture, as explained in another section.
6. Moisten all substances into the wake of a wrung-out sponge.
7. Distribute a 1/4-inch-thick (6.35 millimeter) layer of cardboard or paper along with this compost/manure coating. Lay it down with rocks, bricks, or shovels of dirt to prevent it from blowing off as you operate.
8. Scrub the paper coating entirely with plain water.
9. Instead of using this coating after you distribute it, then you can soak your paper/cardboard at a bathtub of water before dispersing it.
10. Distribute 6 inches (15 centimeters) of straw at the upper coating, watering it because you work to make sure moisture during.

Planting in sheet mulch beds

Once constructing your layers of organic matter as I explain in the previous section, you are ready to plant.

1. Pull aside the straw to make a pit the size of the fist.
2. Use a trowel to cut a gap at the paper/cardboard coating. In the event the cardboard or paper is inflexible, use a utility knife to cut it through. This opening allows potential plant roots to spread unimpeded.
3. Fill the pot with a couple or two of dirt from a present backyard (dig some dirt in the landscape in case you don't have a backyard). Soil harbors zillions of neighborhood decomposer organisms prepared to begin breaking down organic matter in your new garden.
4. Sow seeds or transplant seedlings into the ground.
5. Water and nourish them required in almost any garden situation.

Planting next season's garden

In a year, your natural thing layers will probably have broken, and you can turn the sheet mulch below to improve the ground. As an alternative, you might also utilize this permaculture sheet construction process as an authentic"-no-till" process of dirt construction. Only reconstruct the layers, as explained in the prior section, "Building garden dirt" to repeat this procedure after year without turning into the compost beneath.

10 FAQS ABOUT COMPOST

Not a lot of decades back, most people with a little yard grew a few of their creations and generally had a mulch pile nearby for enhancing their garden land. Composting was something that we simply knew how to do, and children absorbed the ability by turning the heap or functioning in the backyard as a portion of the actions! But, composting knowledge appears to have dropped by the wayside for most people, in the event the amount of questions I have fielded is some sign. If you are a newbie in regards to composting, the subsequent fast answers to typically asked questions will probably get you up to speed and willing to dig.

What's Compost? Truly?

Compost is a combination of decayed and decaying organic substances. Though like compost, humus is a natural thing that has attained its final state of decomposition. Compost might be put on top of the ground as compost, but other natural mulches, like bark or wood chips, are not adequately decomposed to be contemplated mulch. You enhance your garden beds with the addition of compost since it helps maintain nutrients and moisture from sandy soil and also improves drainage and aeration in clay dirt. Irrespective of soil type, compost improves soil structure and supplies nourishment to crops. It's possible to make compost readily from lawn wastes, kitchen scraps, and household waste like cardboard and paper.

Which Are Browns and Greens?

Composters refer to the natural thing that is saturated in carbon as browns and substance that is high in nitrogen. Carbon materials for composting contain tender leaves, sterile plant trimmings, paper, cardboard, paper, along with sawdust. Grass clippings, spent garden crops, vegetable and fruit scraps, coffee grounds, tea bags, and manure are all nitrogen resources. When mixing a batch of mulch, mix around three parts brownish with a single green.

Could I Compost All My Toilet Scraps? How about Pet Waste?

If it has to do with compostable materials and everything can and can not move on your heap or bin, then it is not a free-for-all. Do not place meat, fish, bones, milk, oils, or dirt on your compost bin or pile. They can turn rancid and moldy and might bring in pests, like dogs, rodents, foxes, raccoons, and many others.

Never place kitty, dog pet waste on your mulch. It might contain pathogens that may be transmitted to people.

Can I Need to Obtain a Container into Compost?

Organic matter does not rust into a container. It decomposes as well at a freestanding pile aboveground or within a hole in the floor. But a container is now a far more efficient utilization of distance and makes it a lot easier to generate compost quicker should you keep its contents. You can fashion a bark container out of recycled stuff that costs nothing, or even next-to-nothing, based upon your scavenging abilities. For example, four transport pallets make a compost bin that is pretty darn near the perfect size.

Check with your region's reliable waste control center for accessibility of complimentary used trash cans jammed as composters. A few of those agencies may also provide fabricated containers at a lower cost to promote composting organic things in the home instead of sending it into a landfill.

Can I Switch Compost Often?

Nope. Some beautiful day, have a rest from your hectic schedule, and proceed to get an entry through the forests. You won't find legions of Mother Nature's minions turning off organic thing with pitchforks. Still, the forest floor is covered with beautiful, black humus. The decomposition procedure is continuing all about us whether we engage. Provided that you are in no rush to acquire finished mulch, don't hesitate to heap it up and allow it to rust on its schedule.

How Long before Organic Matter Becomes Compost?

"It depends" is your fast (although maybe not illuminating) response. Factors impacting the rate of decomposition comprise the mixture of nitrogen and carbon substances, how little the portions are, moisture content, aeration from the heap, and also the temperature of this season. Generally, plan to a mean of 31/2 to 6 weeks to reach usable compost. This period assumes you begin with a proper ratio of sliced or shredded green (nitrogen) and brown (carbon) components, which you moisten each of the organic things as you construct a heap at least one cubic yard (1 cubic meter) in dimension. If you flip this heap a few days to aerate and add moisture needed, you are going to harvest some compost in just two weeks! Throw any undecomposed bits back in a pile or to a new heap to break down farther.

Getting mulch in as few as four or three months can also be entirely possible. Start outside as I explain in the previous paragraph, then monitor the heap's daily temperatures, turning it around four days to coincide with fever drops.

How Can I Know When My Compost Is about to Work With?

Finished compost is dark brown -- almost black -- in the shade. Its feel is more loose, crumbly, and uniform in size. The majority of the first ingredients are now unrecognizable. (If you can find any more significant chunks of substances that have not completely decomposed, throw them in a fresh pile to divide in another round.)

If you have been keeping a sexy heap, the composted material will not reheat after turning after it is ready to work with. Should you squeeze a handful of compost, then it ought to be damp. The finished compost smells earthy and beautiful. Cannot I Send My Yard and Household Waste into a Landfill into Decompose? Why all the fuss of composting at home? It could surprise you since it did me the very first time that I read it about; however, natural materials do not decompose exceptionally well in a landfill. Heavy equipment cleans and packs the refuse tightly that the majority of the atmosphere is made out. With oxygen, aerobic decomposer organisms can not perform their job. Garbologists, scientists who examine what happens to the planet's trash, have dug into the depths of landfills to discover perfectly understandable old papers and identifiable (although likely not quite enticing) food things. Besides, there are sustainability problems regarding the hills of garbage humans generate for landfills. Trucks and heavy-equipment burn gas and create air pollution while dispersing and depriving the refuse. Many people have fulfilled their capability, and there is too little room to construct more (nobody needs a landfill in their yard). And remember that methane gas, a culprit in global warming, is a byproduct of landfills.

Could I Compost in Winter?

Yes, composting can happen throughout the year. As temperatures cool, the more faster-working mesophilic and thermophilic microorganisms will slough off and also the cool-loving, however, slower-acting psychrophiles will require over. It is also possible to insulate your heap with a thick coating of leaves, straw, or sod to allow it to keep warm through winter. A few decompositions will happen; however, things will perk up as temperatures warm.

Could I Use Compost rather than Fertilizer?

Compost is known as a soil change or improver as opposed to a fertilizer. Since your mulch's nutrient levels vary significantly from batch to batch as a result of the first ingredients and procedure of decomposition, it is not possible to understand what nutrients it includes without even examining. Nevertheless, most compost includes a vast array of nutrients, including trace elements, to encourage wholesome plant development, so adding mulch for the garden most surely enhances soil fertility.

11 TIPS FOR TROUBLE SHOOTING COMPOST

Composting is a somewhat simple activity because decomposition proceeds whether you fuss on your fundamental issue. However, if something does not look quite right for you, this chapter will offer the ideas that you want to acquire your composting campaigns back on a course or alleviate your worries.

Slow Decomposition

I inform you of the way organic matter decomposes to create mulch in Chapter 3, but just like so many things in existence, decomposition does not always go according to plan. Several aspects can impede down the decomposition of your mulch. This list covers a few of the more important causes and methods to fight them:

◊ nsufficient humidity: A fast-decomposing mulch pile comprises 40 to 60 percent water. A couple of organic matter ought to feel moist, such as a wrung-out sponge.

◊ Low nitrogen: Organic thing ought to be approximately just one part nitrogen (green) substance to three components carbon (brownish) substance. Greens are sometimes in short supply when heaps become constructed, or they float so fast that you want to include more nitrogen substances afterward.

◊ Too much or too small mass: The top pile size for optimum decomposition involves three cubic feet (3 ft tall x 3 ft wide x 3 ft deep, approximately one cubic meter) plus five cubic feet (1.5 cubic meters). At this dimension, the heap can self-insulate and keep heat and dampness, but it is not so big that airflow into the center is obstructed.

◊ Poor aeration: The aboveground efficient decomposer organisms require oxygen to flourish. As oxygen from the heap is drained, decomposition slows. Turning the heap occasionally incorporates oxygen. You might even add aeration tubes once you construct a heap to boost airflow.

◊ Cold climate: Even the many active decomposer organisms operate in hot temperatures. To enhance heat retention through chilly weather, raise the heap dimension, insulate the outer borders of your heap with thick layers of leaves, or sod, or protect it with a tarp.

Hovering Swarms of Teeny Flies

The fleas that you may sometimes see swarming on your mulch pile are precisely the same vinegar flies that you will find congregating inside about a bowl of fruit.

All these gnat-like flies are benign, though you may consider them a hassle. Gardeners in the U.K. telephone them flies, and also in the USA, they go by the title of fruit flies. Female vinegar flies lay eggs on fruit and vegetable skins, along with the hatching larvae feed on the parasites found in fruits and veggies. To control these underground luxuries, bury kitchen bits and food waste deeply inside the compost heap. When incorporating kitchen waste into a present heap, pay it with an inch of dirt, also a few inches of warm, brown stuff, like straw or leaves.

Fat, White Grubs

The fat, white grubs you will unearth on your heap, are the creatures of different scarab beetles, including Japanese beetles, June beetles, or dung beetles. Even the grubs have six arms and darker colored heads, which range from tan to red-orange. They flourish in the moist glow of your mulch pile, feeding and breaking rotting organic matter, making them valuable indeed. Should you choose, handpick the grubs and also leave them out in the open just as a skillet for birds.

In the majority of humid climates, all these grubs are not known to pose substantial problems to plants. Nonetheless, in different ponds, a few species have become dangerous pests that consume and destroy the root systems of lawns and agricultural plants. If you think your grub people are from the command or guess that the grubs are harmful to other crops, check with your county cooperative extension office or local nursery to determine which species reside in your town and how to manage them.

Dead Vermicomposting Worms

Worms absolutely, positively needs to be surrounded with moist bedding. If bedding starts, their skin dries out, plus they perish. A general rule is to keep bedding a minimum of 8 inches (20 centimeters) deep, which gets the dampness of a wrung-out sponge. Food scraps can offer extra moisture; however, you might also spray additional water onto your heap periodically. Worms do not wish to reside in a woods, however, so be mindful about moisture. An appropriate food source additionally keeps your vermicomposting worms living and squirming. Your worms will have their bedding in case no more food scraps are all readily available. For the entire scoop on vermicomposting and maintaining your worms living and well, take a look at 10.

A Lot of Bugs Crawling Around

Relax, sit back and Revel in the show! You see several nature's decomposers on the job. Bugs are an indication that all is well on your compost realm.

In addition to countless germs you can not see without a microscope, observable macroorganisms occupy your heap to break down organic matter. Familiar mulch pile denizens contain pillbugs (crawlers) and springtails (jumpers). Read more on the subject of decomposer organisms in Chapter 3.

Ammonia Odor

A nicely assembled and managed compost heap doesn't smell. A powerful ammonia odor is usually due to an excessive amount of nitrogen (greens). Whenever there's an overabundance of oxygen, the decomposer organisms can not process it quickly enough, and also the surplus nitrogen is discharged to the air as ammonia. Extra moisture in a heap may also bring about an ammonia odor. Turn the heap and include more carbon-rich substances, like dry leaves, straw, shredded paper, or sawdust. In the event, you buy mulch in mass, and it smells of ammonia, then allow it to grow further before employing.

Rotten Egg Odor

I replicate a correctly constructed and controlled compost heap doesn't smell! If you encounter a rotten egg odor, then heap contents have become compressed, compacted, or overly moist. When air can not penetrate, aerobic decomposers disappear off, and their cerebral cousins presume control. Anaerobic decomposers provide off musty hydrogen sulfide gas as a portion of the attempts. That is why landfills odor bad -- full gear compacts the deny, and anaerobic composting organisms do all of the work. On your mulch pile, you are very likely to possess matted grass clippings, globs of new mulch, slurry-like toilet waste, or alternative high-nitrogen pockets. Introduce additional oxygen by merely turning the whole heap, and include dried leaves, straw, or paper to soak up extra moisture as necessary.

Slurry-Like Compost

When your compost is too lean and liquid, then the cause might become your compost pile surroundings or its components. Cover open freestanding or bins piles using a waterproof tarp. Should you reside in a rainy climate, then think about an enclosed container (see Chapter 5). In case you've got a covered bin or heap and the consequences of the compost gets too moist, spread it around the floor to wash out or mix this up with much more sterile, bulky brown fabrics, like wood chips, straw, and sawdust.

Eek! A sword at the Compost

Mice seek worm, sticky organic substances to construct their nests. Length of leaves and straw, mainly when flipped infrequently, are ideal in the mouse's view. To discourage rodents, turn open heaps frequently and purge materials thoroughly.

Rats in and about the heap are more problematic since they might spread the disease to people. Do not add possibly rat-attracting beef, bones, grease, oils, fats, or milk products to mulch piles. You could even mulch within an enclosed container to keep out vermin. Read more about pest-proofing your bins in Chapter 5.

Animals Scattering Compost

Do not place meat, fish, bones, milk, oil, or dirt on your heap, which might bring animal insects. If you mulch additional kitchen bits, bury them in the middle of the heap. As an alternative, you could cover kitchen bits with an inch of soil or finished compost, then coating a couple of inches of sterile stuff in addition to If the issue persists, switch into an animal-proof enclosed bin using a secure top and underside. Chapter 5 provides suggestions on maintaining critters from crap containers without any Coping with decomposition.

12 CONCLUSION

Gardens are once more coming into vogue. As well as people begin to cultivate their veggies, they're starting to recognize the worth of high-quality soil that is packed with nourishment. The higher your land is, the fitter and more profitable your crops will be. To put it differently, build it, and they'll come. It is the area where composting comes from.

Composting is both the science and art of mixing organic substances with air and water, so the nourishment in the organic matter decomposes to a plant-useable type known as humus.
Regrettably, a lot of the info regarding composting you see in books and magazines, while accurate, is overly complicated. Discerning the carbon to carbon dioxide each time you throw stuff to your mulch pile, measuring pH levels, and carrying the heap's temperatures are unquestionably optional pursuits.

The reality is that composting is all about as straightforward as it gets. Anyone using a spare half an hour plus a few organic materials lying about could start to reap its advantages. It isn't rocket science. You do not have to wait for a specific period of the year to begin. You do not need to purchase any expensive equipment. And you do not have to do a lick on mathematics.

The secret is to get some advice available (this publication), decide as to what sort of containers or bin you'd love to utilize, then go out and begin a heap. You may produce a perfectly decent heap in 30 minutes--and generally less. But if you are like most people, as soon as you begin reaping the advantages of your very first easy heap, you are going to be willing to try your hands at distinct techniques in a bid to receive as much compost as possible, as fast as possible. This publication is meant to develop with you and your backyard as you research the many approaches to make organic waste materials to gold.